B
Power

Brain Power

THE 12-WEEK MENTAL TRAINING PROGRAMME

Marilyn vos Savant

and Leonore Fleischer

piatkus

PIATKUS

First published in the US and Canada as *Brain Building*
First published in Great Britain in 1992 by Piatkus Books Ltd
This paperback edition published in 2009 by Piatkus

Grateful acknowledgement is made to reprint passages from 'How to
Read a Book' copyright © 1972 by Mortimer J. Adler and Charles van
Doren, reprinted by permission of Simon and Schuster, Inc., and 'The
Brain' by Richard Restak, M.D. published by Bantam Books

A CIP catalogue record for this book
is available from the British Library

ISBN 978-0-7499-4121-5

Printed and bound in Great Britain by
CPI Mackays, Chatham, ME5 8TD

Papers used by Piatkus are natural, renewable and recyclable
products sourced from well-managed forests and certified
in accordance with the rules of the Forest Stewardship Council.

Mixed Sources
Product group from well-managed
forests and other controlled sources
www.fsc.org   Cert no. SGS-COC-004081
© 1996 Forest Stewardship Council

Piatkus
An imprint of
Little, Brown Book Group
100 Victoria Embankment
London EC4Y 0DY

An Hachette UK Company
www.hachette.co.uk

www.piatkus.co.uk

CONTENTS

FOREWORD

Your mind is the heart and spirit of your life. It is the one thing that can never be taken from you and the one thing that you can never give away. It is always yours, under your control. Build it, and you build the workings of your future. Let it stagnate, and you live in the past.

Whoever told you that you cannot increase your intelligence? Whoever taught you not to try? They didn't know.

Flex your mind. Develop it. Use it. It will enrich you and bring you the love of life that thrives on truth and understanding.

This book helps enormously. It contains the distilled methods of one of the world's most effective thinkers, Marilyn vos Savant. Practical, direct methods, applicable by you to build your brainpower. And they are indeed methods to incorporate into your way of thinking and into your daily perception of reality that can vastly improve your mind.

The essence of *Brain Power* is the taking of active control of your thought processes—developing mental tools to approach difficult problems in an effective fashion, freeing yourself from false assumptions and the mental hammerlock that lack of self-confidence and over-reliance on authoritarian opinion can have on you. You will learn to think with more clarity and with greater precision. You will learn to trust yourself. And as you achieve that trust, your intelligence will expand and your interests will broaden.

Marilyn vos Savant is my wife. During our first year together, I felt that she had opened my eyes, expanded my outlook, improved my mind—but I didn't know just how it was happening. It was much more than love alone. She didn't show me the manuscript for *Brain Power* until the final draft was completed, although we had often talked about the project. As I read it, I recognized one idea after another that she lives with and also had imparted to me, ideas that we now live with together, about open-mindedness, objectivity, intellectual honesty, and strength. I saw them gathered together, organized, worked into the format of an educational manual. *Brain Power* is a workbook. And I was delighted to find in it so much of what I had been learning from her.

So I asked if I might write this foreword. Even if you doubt that you can improve your intelligence, you surely know that you can improve your mind. Believe in yourself, and you are likely to do both. Stay with it, work at it hard, and you will gain ever so much more. That has been my experience with the artificial heart. At times it may seem impossible, but it isn't. The only way to success is through persistence and hard work. The only efforts that can command all your energies are those that are really worthwhile. Your own mind is one of them.

—Robert Jarvik, M.D.

PREFACE

Just as the human body can be strengthened and toned to muscular power through bodybuilding exercise, so too the mind can be strengthened and sharpened through a program of Brain Building. Specific bodybuilding exercises are designed for specific muscles, making them work, stretch, and break through old limits to new, more supple, frontiers. Brain Building works exactly that way on your intelligence, stretching and shaping your mind and bringing you to new heights of intellectual fitness.

The key to any exercise is habit, the constant repetition that makes it second nature—as automatic perhaps as breathing. For the next twelve weeks, I am going to help you build your mental muscles in the same way by showing you how to develop the habit of thinking. The Brain Building program is a "trimester," something like a school term. Begin right now, and in twelve weeks you will acquire and learn to use the tools and techniques of power thinking.

As in any college trimester, Brain Building is a course that requires interaction between student and instructor, and you'll find plenty of opportunities to test your progress through the course. In some parts of this book, the exercises are simple; in other chapters, they may pose some difficulty. Be assured that the logic behind both the simple and complex exercises is the same—to show you how to build your perceptions, sharpen your intellect, and open your eyes to new ways of thinking. With this book, I am going to surprise you and demand that you think in ways you've never thought before.

Remember, time is the most precious commodity we have, and under the stresses and pressures of everyday contemporary life, we often trade it for less than its real value. Everything we do is time-consuming, but very few things are time-repaying. I believe that building your brain power is one of them. With the principles of Brain Building mastered, you'll have the mental tools to make every moment count, to set your priorities and stick to them, to pay out your mental energies only for what repays you in productivity, satisfaction, reduced stress, and a better life.

I think you'll find the Brain Building program stimulating, challenging, and fun. It is up to you to make the exercises work by incorporating them into your daily routine, making them a habit for a lifetime of improvement. You won't need any special equipment—a pad of paper, a pencil, some books, a newspaper, your everyday world. You already possess the two specialized and irreplaceable pieces of equipment necessary: your own brain and this book. If you make good use of them, I can with confidence promise you this:

The Brain Building twelve-week program will help you develop your intelligence and unlock the almost-limitless power of your intellect, your perceptions, and your understanding. You will be able to bring these newfound, newly-developed skills and techniques to bear on every aspect of your daily life, including problem-solving, decision-making, business, and personal relationships. Once it becomes a habit, the technique of Brain Building will be yours forever, your own permanent key to thinking better.

—Marilyn vos Savant

CHAPTER 1

THE BRAIN BUILDING PROGRAM

| M | T | W | T | F | S | S |

Twelve Weeks to a Stronger Intelligence

I didn't want to write this book.

But I was talked into it by one of my dearest friends. "You know, Marilyn," he said to me, "you're the only person I know who's both physically and mentally fit."

Well, I protested that, all right. It's true that I go to the gym every two or three days, but I'm certainly not a body-builder, and I don't *want* to be one.

"That's the excuse people use for not working out at all," he commented.

That gave me pause. NOBODY WANTS TO BE A BOOK-WORM, EITHER, BUT IS THAT AN EXCUSE FOR NEVER WORKING OUT WITH YOUR MIND AT ALL? An unfit mind is as unattractive as an unfit body. Even more so.

"You should tell people that they can have both if they make the effort."

But who am I to tell people? I'm listed in the *Guinness Book of World Records* under "highest I.Q.," but people assume that's "natural" because of my surname, which means "wise man." My grandmother's last name was "Savant" even *before* she married my grandfather, whose last name happened to be "vos Savant."

"Sure," he said. "But remind them that there are thousands of people named Einstein, too, but we've only heard of one of them."

But I just don't have the *time* for it. I write the "Ask Marilyn" question-and-answer column for *Parade* Magazine, which has a circulation of 32,000,000 and a readership of 64,000,000, the largest in the world. I'm working on a political fantasy detailing life in the United States 200 years from now, and I'm putting together a collection of humorous short stories, too. And when I'm not writing, I lecture to businesses and universities.

"I guess you're busier than I thought."

You bet I'm busy. And I'm married to Robert Jarvik, M.D., the inventor of the artificial heart that bears his name. That takes all the *rest* of the time.

So, I teamed up with my coauthor and wrote this book. And here it is.

How to Exercise Your Way to Mental Fitness

Brain Building is a program of exercise: mental exercise. Like any such program, it's *cumulative*, which means that for maximum effect, you must expand the program and build on the exercises, adding new exercises to the ones you have already mastered. Think of a typical exercise program for overall body toning, and you'll see what I mean. You begin with a few minutes of stretches, to warm up and loosen the muscles. Then you might learn a set of exercises for the upper arms and shoulders and later, another for the legs, still more exercises for the lower back, and a different set for strengthening the chest and upper torso. You *add* these exercises gradually, but without discarding the ones you already do easily. So a workout program might start with ten minutes of exercises, and by the end of the second week, you could be up to thirty minutes.

By the end of the month, you could be doing a sixty-minute workout using *all* the exercises you've learned.

The same goes for this program. *Brain Power* gives you the means by which you can gradually strengthen every area of your thinking until, at the end of the book, you should be following the entire program easily and naturally, getting maximum results.

Before you dive into this book headfirst, take a little warm-up time. Remember that you can't build a great body in a few hours; the same goes for your intellect. Don't speed-read *Brain Power* or try to cram all its ideas into your head at once. Remember that the secret to the success of any exercise program is *repetition, repetition, repetition,* until the exercise becomes second nature to you. Only then will you begin to see results.

The more time you spend with any of these chapters, the more slowly you read through it, and the more frequently you reread and refer back to it, the more helpful it will become. As you do the exercises, you will find some of them more gratifying than others—which ones are better for any individual person will vary from reader to reader. For example, you may already possess an aptitude for logic and mathematics, so perhaps the communications-building exercises will be of most benefit to you. You may already possess a finely honed and well-sharpened set of vocabulary tools, but you might approach problem-solving in an illogical manner now; work on the logic chapter a little harder. If the results of the warm-up quiz in the third chapter show that your mind could use a bit of expanding and that your eyes need opening to the world around you, make that your first priority.

Become aware of how you are thinking right now—how you arrive at opinions and make decisions. This self-awareness is the first step in Brain Building. The quiz I call "George the Warm-up" will help you reach an awareness of how your own special, individual mind operates.

The next two chapters will deal in depth with the human brain and human intelligence; these sections will be followed by perhaps the most unusual quiz you've ever taken. After that, the Brain Building exercises begin. Some of them are surprisingly easy; some may be trickier than they first appear. Each chapter will explain a different aspect of intelligence and how it can be enhanced and strengthened.

We'll start off slow and easy, building your vocabulary. You'll work with what is familiar to you—your everyday reading of newspapers and magazines. What this chapter will do for you (in addition to bringing you new skill with words) is to teach you how to take note of something new, how not to pass over the unknown without trying to know it, and how to use reference books to look up what you don't know.

After vocabulary, *Brain Power* moves to the challenging exercises in mathematics and logic to prepare the mental ground for everything else to come. I hope to show you the beauty and simplicity of precise thinking and how important it is to you and to the rest of the program. Logic is the foundation of correct thinking—it is dispassionate and not tinged by emotions. Armed with the weapon of logic, you can now forge ahead boldly into new areas of thinking and problem-solving.

Next, the Brain Building program turns from the general to the specific, to the inner you—your insight and intuition, your orientation, the strengthening of your attention span and physical senses. Brain Building in these areas will give you confidence in your mental abilities and the confidence to proceed to those outer areas in which you are in daily touch with the world around you—communication, information, comprehension, and perspective.

Generally speaking, each section works as follows: I'll define a specific area of intelligence, either theoretical or practical: verbal skills, for example, or mathematics. Then I'll provide you with a series of Brain Builders plus exercises demonstrating their use. Most of the exercises may be done at any time of the day along with and as a part of your customary activities. Some will require a special time set aside for them. Some are simple "dos" and others are simple "don'ts." Each of the Brain Builders in any given area of intelligence is designed to stretch that area, to work it out, and to exercise that part of your intelligence until it's stronger.

4

Stay with the exercises you find difficult until you've mastered them. The tougher they are, the more they will stretch your brain and build it. Although the program is geared to twelve weeks of straight read-through, people learn different things at different rates. Brains vary, and so do intelligences, thank goodness, or we'd all be grinding out the same thoughts in the same monotonous way.

You, for instance, may find it easier to keep repeating the program. These repetitions may take you days or weeks or even months. If you don't get it all in twelve weeks, don't get impatient, and don't worry. Let one set of exercises become as natural to you as breathing before you progress to the next. The book will wait; it will still be there for you when you're ready to read on.

Read this book slowly, and think of the exercises as doors opening up unused rooms in your mind. Stop and reflect; the more often you do this, the more *Brain Power* will be of use to you.

Increase the frequency of the exercises until they become part of your daily routine. As with a physical exercise program, this becomes easier as you practice. Go back and reread the pages you don't fully understand.

Write your comments in the margins of this book. If at all possible, talk to somebody else who is reading *Brain Power* or who has already read it. It's like jogging with a friend; you both benefit, and it makes the tougher going a little easier.

CHAPTER 2

WEEK ONE: MONDAY—WEDNESDAY

| M | T | W | L | L | L | L |

The Brain—Not an Organ of Minor Importance

TOOLS YOU WILL NEED FOR WEEK ONE:
A photograph of yourself; a large, hand-held mirror; pencil;
paper; a pocket dictionary; some quiet time to read and to take
two short tests and a longer one.

"The seat of the soul and the control of voluntary movement—in
fact, of nervous functions in general—are to be sought in the
heart. The brain is an organ of minor importance."

Thus wrote Aristotle, the fourth century B.C. Greek philosopher, zoologist, and classifier of animal species; Aristotle
the tutor of Alexander the Great; Aristotle the author of
some of history's earliest scientific and political treatises;
Aristotle who, more than a thousand years after his death,
was still referred to as "he himself," because he needed no
other introduction. This very same Aristotle turned up his
Grecian nose at the brain. An "organ or minor importance,"
was his haughty Aristotelian opinion.

6

An Overview of the Brain

For centuries we've understood that "he himself" was way off base, that, in fact, the opposite is true. The heart is simply a biological pump that brings oxygen flowing into our cells to keep tissue alive. It is the brain that controls movement, both voluntary and involuntary. Passion begins in the brain; so does love, hate, pain, fear, wonder, imagination, inspiration, enthusiasm, apathy, speculation, mistrust, honor, a sense of humor, a craving for rocky road ice cream, and all other thoughts and feelings. The brain runs the show, from the involuntary intake and outgo of breath to the voluntary embrace of a beloved friend.

Yet, every February 14th, we send out greeting cards honoring a pump. Throughout the ages, the metaphor for our valentine has remained the heart; nobody remembers to say "thank you" to the brain, even though Shakespeare struck closer to the mark when he asked, in *The Merchant of Venice:*

> Tell me where is fancy bred,
> Or in the heart or in the head . . . ?

Heredity or Environment or Both?

The human brain has been the subject of fascinated scientific study even before Aristotle chose to disdain it. Yet even with the latest developments in laser technology and the miracle of microchips, the brain remains a largely enigmatic study, some of its functions still a mystery. Are the brain and the intelligence one and the same thing? Is the brain merely a physical organ while intelligence is something intangible, something science may never fathom? Which is more important to the development of the intelligence, heredity or environment? Or is there something else, something more important than either, or even both together?

What is the reason that some of us are able to visualize a long series of future moves on a chessboard while others find it hard to foresee the consequences of their very next move? Why are some people strategists and others tacticians?

Why, if environment plays as important a role in brain development among humans as scientists claim it does, are the actual, physical brains of a Wall Street broker, a post-Impressionist painter, and a Kalahari desert bushman virtually indistinguishable from one another? What is the nature of talent, and why are some talented people artistic while others show a mathematical or scientific bent? Are our very personalities and natures only the by-products of chemical neurotransmissions and electrical connections going on in a mass of pinkish-gray organic matter?

These secrets and others are still locked within a three-pound organ inside your skull: the brain.

What exactly is the brain? What defines it? Let's take a brief look at the thing itself, its components, and its composition.

A Warm-up Exercise to Start You Off

Here is a "stretch-and-tone" kind of preliminary warm-up to your first Brain Building exercise, just to loosen up your mental muscles.

Try this: As you read about the brain, stop from time to time and "take a look." Pick up your mirror and look at your own head. Envision the very fiber of your being just inside the protective skull. With each area of the brain I discuss, try to locate it on your own head using the mirror and running your hand over the part of the skull where it's located. Your accuracy in locating the area is less important than your realization that those brain areas are not only a reality in this book but inside your own head. The purpose of this easy exercise is for you to *make the connection between the words you are reading with the immediacy of reality.*

Ready? Go.

The Central Nervous System

The central nervous system is divided into two parts—a group of nerve cells inside the head and a group of nerve cells inside the spinal cord.

If you could take the top of your skull off and look inside, you'd see, under three membranes and a quantity of cerebrospinal fluid, a large, convoluted mass resembling a shelled walnut, only a lot softer.

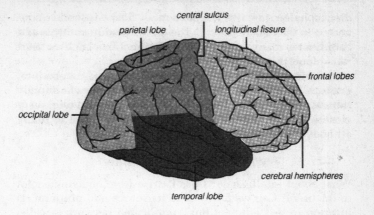

central sulcus

parietal lobe   longitudinal fissure

frontal lobes

occipital lobe

cerebral hemispheres

temporal lobe

This is the brain, and it's a far more complex organ than any superficial examination could reveal. It is composed of two major sections, the left and right *cerebral hemispheres*, which are almost, but not quite, mirror images of each other. Each of these hemispheres is composed in turn of four sections, the *frontal lobe*, the *parietal lobe*, the *occipital lobe*, and the *temporal lobe*. Separating these hemispheres and lobes are three fissures that look almost like crevasses within mountain ranges—the *longitudinal fissure*, the *sylvian fissure*, and the *central sulcus*. That's its topology.

How does the brain function? The central nervous system is composed of the *spinal cord*, the *brain stem*—which includes the *medulla, pons, midbrain*, and *diencephalon*—the *cerebellum*, and what neuroscientists call the *cerebral hemispheres*. Let's begin at the tail end, with your spinal cord, which takes in information from your skin and muscles and sends out signals for movement. The upper extension of the spinal cord is called the brain stem. The brain stem receives similar information from the head and neck area and processes it accordingly. It is the home base of all our senses with the exception of smell and vision. Vision travels directly into the *cerebral cortex*, and smell travels directly into the *limbic system*.

Within the brain stem, we find that the medulla (sometimes called the medulla oblongata) leads to the pons, the pons leads to the midbrain, and the midbrain leads to the diencephalon, just like the old song—"The headbone's connected to the neckbone . . ." The diencephalon controls and coordinates many important bodily functions such as heart rate, blood pressure, and respiration.

Covering the pons and the midbrain is the cerebellum. Beneath the cerebral hemispheres is the overwhelmingly intricate mass of *basal ganglia*. The basal ganglia work very closely with the cerebellum; together they control virtually all body coordination.

What Exactly Is Intelligence?

What about intelligence? Does it arise from one single spot in the brain? Can we follow it to its source and pinpoint its location in this efficient but complicated network of cells, chemicals and fluids? The twin cerebral hemispheres control humankind's highest functions—those cognitive, ideational, and imaginative functions, the intelligence. The cerebral hemispheres may then be called the true home of our inner cosmos: our minds.

How does this vastly complex system work? It functions in the body as we do in the world, through *communication*, through signals sent from one cell in the brain to the next. A single nerve cell in the brain consists of the cell body itself, one long fiber, and a variety of branching fibers. Nerve signals are sent from the cell body down the path of the long fiber and out through the branches. Synapses are the link between nerve cells.

The Brain's Building Block: The Neuron

The brain's fundamental unit, its building block, is the neuron, which is another name for a nerve cell. Historically, scientists were divided into two opposing groups regarding neuron communication. One faction contended that signals traveled by electrical impulses; the opposing faction held that they traveled by chemical transmitters. Today, these groups have agreed that neither position was entirely wrong and that communication within the brain is electrochemical.

"Each of the at least ten billion neurons in the human brain may have over a thousand synapses—points of contact between nerve cells," writes Richard Restak, M.D., in his book *The Brain* (Bantam, 1984). "With some cells within the cerebral cortex, the numbers may approach two hundred thousand connections. The total number of connections within the vast network of the brain's neuronal system is truly astronomical—*greater than the number of particles in the known universe.*" I have added italics to point up the overwhelming complexity of that miraculous organ, the brain.

Yet, even today, there are a radical few who would disagree with the popular electrical-connection theory. Richard Bergland, M.D., a prominent neurosurgeon, writes in his book *The Fabric of Mind* (Viking Press, 1986),

> There is now little doubt that the brain is a gland; it produces hormones, it has hormone receptors, it is bathed in hormones, hormones run up and down the fibres of individual nerves, and every activity that the brain is engaged in involves hormones. The implications of this are immense, not only for those who think about thinking—philosophers and scientists—but for virtually every intellectual who reveres the mysterious workings of the mind. Most unsettling to established dogma is the realization that regulatory hormones—the new stuff of thought—are found all over the body. Can thinking go on outside the brain? Much scientific evidence points to that disturbing, previously unthinkable possibility.

But whether the brain is transmitter or gland, whether thinking goes on inside the skull alone or, as Dr. Bergland seems to suggest, elsewhere in the body, we come into this world with only a very few innate forms of behavior. Nearly everything else we do we *learn* to do. But what exactly is learning? One good definition might be that learning is what allows us to make sense of the confusing array of stimuli that reach us from every part of our environment.

Trading Places

Let us go back for a moment to those look-alike, function-alike physical brains of the stockbroker, the painter, and the Kalahari desert-dweller, each of whom possesses a unique mind-set and functions in an environment different from that of the other two. Imagine the stockbroker set down in the middle of the bushman's desert, the painter finding herself on the floor of the Exchange at the height of trading, and the bushman magically transported to the modern Pompidou museum in Paris.

The skill of picking high-yield stocks and bonds is not a useful one in the desert; there, finding food and locating water is paramount. But food and water are not the issue in an art museum; an entirely different set of stimuli are present, and our bushman has so far learned no way to function. Meanwhile, the artist will almost certainly be at a loss in the hectic and frantic world of puts and calls, unable to earn her living, her senses assaulted from every side. Here are three equally intelligent humans suddenly faced with vastly different environments. How will they cope?

Let's leave our trio hanging over a cliff for the moment because I want you to try another stretch-and-tone warm-up exercise right here:

The Stranger in Your Mirror

Pick up your mirror and look only at your face. Pretend that you don't know yourself and that the image in the glass isn't you. Concentrate on the mirror. Is there anything you can objectively see in the reflected face that tells you whether the face belongs to a stockbroker, an artist, or (putting color aside) a Kalahari bushman?

No, of course not. The difference is not on the outside, but inside, within the brain itself. Heredity provides us with some predispositions, but never with our professions.

But back now to our hypothetical cliff-hanging situation— three people trapped in alien environments. This can actually be resolved without catastrophe. Given enough time, each of the three has the capacity to learn the skills necessary to survive by first observing, then coming to understand the new environment, and, finally, learning to function within it.

The stockbroker will find water, although he will probably never be the hunter the bushman is. The man from the Kalahari may never learn to appreciate modern painting, but he will learn to move with some ease around his new environment, drinking water from the fountains, and snaring food from the snack bar. The painter will eventually discover the difference between a bull and a bear, although she might not find the financial world of any aesthetic value. The three of them will probably never be as successful in their new worlds as they were in their old, but they would almost certainly *survive*.

A Reflection in (and on) the Mirror

Yet another stretching warm-up for your mind:

Look at a photograph of yourself as you would at a stranger, but imagine that the stranger is the artist, the stockbroker, or the tribesman from the Kalahari desert, only with your features. Now look into your mirror and envision the face you see as each of the three in turn, but pretend that each of them was born to your own mother. What do you really see? Reflect upon your reflection. You should see that you are a human being developed not only by heredity, but by circumstance.

The Environment and Your Brain

The human is the only living creature endowed with the gift to overcome and alter the world around him. Using that gift since the dawn of time, humankind has discovered and/or invented shelter, fire, clothing, agriculture, the domestication of animals, and other more sophisticated means of surmounting the problems of environment.

Its reciprocal—environment plays a role in shaping us; we shape our environment to meet our needs. And we do it with the brain.

Dr. Restak, in his excellent book, *The Brain*, confirms this.

Even more dramatic are the differences in brain organization that can be found between animals raised in deprived vs. enriched environments. Merely adding a few toys to play with, or mazes to run through, leads to an increase in the number of synaptic contacts as well as a thickening of the animal's cerebral cortex. . . . The dependence of brain development on environmental influences should come as no surprise. Even casual observations of animals and humans reveal that an enriched, stimulating environment is conducive to mental agility. Each synapse can be considered a component of an interior world wherein neurons interact with each other in ways dependent on the brain's developmental history, its experiences, the richness of the outside environment, and the variety and complexity of sensory experiences. Throughout life—not just during the first few months—the brain's synaptic organization can be altered by the external environment.

And that external environment includes you. In fact, it includes you more than anyone or anything else. *What we ourselves do is obviously the single most important factor in our environment.*

Who Is the Operator of the Brain You Own?

Your head may be the possessor of your brain, but are you the one who operates it? Are you in control, or is your mind at the mercy of the buffeting, biting winds of life? The secret to a more powerful intelligence is twofold. First, you need to gain control of the raw material—that pinkish-gray matter inside your head on which so much of your life depends. Second, you need to widen your viewpoint to include every perspective; in short, you need to stop seeing through your eyes alone and begin to see through *universal* eyes. The first will make you intellectually strong; the second, intellectually powerful.

Gaining control of your brain is the task of the first part of *Brain Power*; gaining perspective is the function of the second part. By the time you have read this book carefully and integrated the exercises into your life, you will not only have increased your intellectual power, you will be able to apply what you have learned in everyday situations even if you are like a stockbroker set down suddenly in the Kalahari desert.

Building your brain power will open a new frontier beyond which lies an understanding that seems nearly incalculable. Think of the seemingly miraculous events, discoveries, and inventions that have occurred in your lifetime alone. Men and women who were born in the year Wilbur and Orville Wright flew a gasoline-powered, canvas-covered aircraft 120 feet, have lived to see men walking on the moon while the astronauts' audio and video transmissions appeared live on television, relayed by communications space satellites.

We live in an age of organ transplants, three-dimensional photography, and apes who are learning to communicate in human language. Will we live to see a cure for cancer or the postponement of old age? There's a chance we will.

As intricate a mass as your brain is, you are still using only a fraction of its potential power. The human brain can be compared to that tough little ant with the high hopes, carrying a rubber tree plant many times its own weight. Even neuroscientists, who study the brain professionally, cannot place exact limits on the brain's capabilities or even suggest whose brains might have the greatest potential.

However, one thing is certain. You can be smarter tomorrow than you are today. The mind can stretch—it can be strengthened, toned, and conditioned to perform miracles for you. Your mind can carry you into the twenty-first century even before the second millenium arrives.

Brief Quiz

A Brief Quiz on the First Chapter to Take on Wednesday Evening

1 What was Aristotle's reverent nickname?
2 What organ did Aristotle think controlled the mind and body?
3 Where are the two parts of the central nervous system?
4 What is the fundamental nerve cell of the brain?
5 What is the link between nerve cells?
6 If we were able to look even more closely at our brains, is it possible that we might find that there is no significant difference between the normal and the bright?
7 Is there perhaps no real physical difference between the brain of that Kalahari desert-dweller and you?
8 Is there perhaps no real physical difference between your brain capabilities and that of Aristotle's?
9 If Aristotle could state that the brain is an organ of minor importance, could he be wrong about other important things?
10 Could you?

And the Answers

1 "He himself."
2 The heart.
3 Inside the head and inside the spinal cord.
4 A neuron.
5 A synapse.
6 Yes.
7 Yes.
8 Yes.
9 Yes.
10 It's hard to believe, I know, but the answer is "yes."

CHAPTER 3

WEEK ONE: THURSDAY—SATURDAY

T F S

I Think, Therefore, What If ...?

"Much learning does not teach a man to have intelligence."

—Heraclitus

On one of the bottom rungs of the evolutionary ladder perches a classification of flatworms called *planaria*. What sets these worms one step up from the life forms on the rung below them is the fact that they possess a rudimentary central nervous system. It's not much of a system, little more than a relatively uncomplicated kind of central cord and some nerves situated along its length, but it's more than a jellyfish or a paramecium can claim. At least it's a start, the first tentative evolutionary step toward the human brain.

You Are What You Eat (If You're a Worm)

In the 1960s, a group of biologists calling themselves "wormrunners" did some experimenting with flatworms, and they discovered a most remarkable (and scientifically debatable) result. If you *teach* a flatworm something, and he learns it, then you can grind up the "smart" worm and feed it to an uneducated flatworm and the "dumb" worm suddenly knows what you have taught the "smart" one. It can now find food at the exit of a maze although it has never been taught to expect food there and even if it has never been through the maze before. Our planarian pal has apparently learned through its belly, proving that you are whom you eat and giving new meaning to the phrase, "digesting information."

There's probably not a stupendous amount you can actually teach a flatworm—maybe one or two things having to do with recognizing its food supply, such as turning right or turning left in a simple maze with food as a reward. Surely not the multiplication table. But, as Dr. Johnson was once supposed to have observed as he watched a performing poodle strut around on its hind legs, it's not whether he does it well that's remarkable, but that he can do it at all!

Not every scientist agrees with the planaria data. Other biologists have disputed the wormrunners' experiments, but even so, the experiments still stand as a fascinating approach to intelligence—through the side door of invertebrate biology, where learning might be taken directly into the tissues of the central nervous system.

Think how wonderful it would be if, instead of being born as a *tabula rasa*, a blank slate, we could be fed, along with our infant formula, every scrap of the hard-won information possessed by every generation that has gone before! Instead of having to learn the bittersweet lessons of history all over again, we could start, not from square one, but from somewhere in the middle; square ten, say. (Of course, we might also be drinking in all the misinformation and all the disinformation, prejudices, and misconceptions of previous generations, but let's not look at the gloomy side. This is, after all, only a fantasy.)

Yet, would having all this predigested information at its tiny, infant fingertips make the baby any more intelligent?

What You Learn Isn't All You Know

At the beginning of this chapter, I gave you a quotation about the difference between learning information and possessing intelligence. The words are from the philosopher Heraclitus, who spanned the fifth and fourth centuries before Christ. Twenty-five hundred years later, he's still right. You might spend most of your life going to school, reading, looking up facts, acquiring information, and memorizing it. But, although you'll become more informed, in the end it won't make you any smarter. Is a reference library smart? Is a computer with a vast storehouse of voluminous data smart? Is the simple act of digesting and then disgorging information either smart or impressive? No.

Does that go for flatworms as well as humans? Or is learning just a function of the worm's central nervous system, merely a biological response to experimentation? What is the difference between your brain and your intelligence? Is the mind the same thing as the intellect? Should humanity be fed learning in small cut-up pieces, like one flatworm lunching on another?

Intelligence Is What Makes Us Ask "Why?"

As we learned in the previous chapter, the brain is an organ, pure and simple—the same kind of organ for just about everybody on the planet, including our stockbroker, artist, and Kalahari bushman. The mind is that mysterious thing that contains not only the intelligence and the learning, but also the perceptions and the emotions. But it is our intellect—our intelligence—that gives us the capacity to reason, to ask questions, to add three and two, to splice genes, to broadcast by communications satellites, and to send Voyager out past Saturn.

For a good definition of intelligence, let us turn to that most reliable compendium of definitions, *Webster's Third New International Dictionary*, published by Merriam-Webster Co.

Intelligence—a) the faculty of understanding; capacity to know or apprehend. b) the available ability as measured by intelligence tests or by other social criteria to use one's existing knowledge to meet new situations and to solve new problems, to learn, to foresee problems, to use symbols or relationships, to create new relationships, to think abstractly: ability to perceive one's environment, to deal with it symbolically, to deal with it effectively, to adjust to it, to work toward a goal: the degree of one's alertness, awareness, or acuity: ability to use with awareness the mechanism of reasoning whether conceived as a unified intellectual factor or as the aggregate of many intellectual factors or abilities, as intuitive or as analytic, organismic, biological, physiological, psychological, or social in origin or nature. . . .

EXERCISE

Look up the word "intelligence" in your own pocket dictionary and compare it with the longer definition above. See how many differences between them you can find, obvious or subtle.

What is striking about Webster's definition is the word "capacity," which captures the true meaning of the word "intelligence." It is a *potential*, separate and distinct from learning, the brain, or the rest of the mind. It is the usable potential to learn, to profit from experience, to deal with problems and solve them, to improve one's own life and those of others, to speculate on the unknown, and to chart new worlds and explore new horizons.

Another stretch-and-tone warm-up for this chapter:

EXERCISE

Come up with your own very brief (20 words or so) definition of intelligence, and write it down. Put it away where you can find it again easily.

Many anthropologists used to believe that Homo sapiens was set apart from (and by this they meant superior to) other species because man was the only animal to make and use tools—Man the Toolmaker, they termed him rather smugly. But in the last thirty years, the research of such scientists as Dr. Jane Goodall have proved that chimpanzees regularly use tools in food-gathering and even as weapons. Other mammals, and even birds, have been observed making use of whatever they can find to extend their reach, augment their strength, or improve their chances of survival. So much for Man the Toolmaker as a unique being.

No, what really separates the human from the animal is the fact that ours is the only species that asks questions. Why? How? And, perhaps the most important question in scientific progress, "What if . . . ?" Humans are curious about everything from the ellipses of planetary orbits to the lifestyles of the rich and famous. To that curiosity, that speculative "What if . . . ?" we can attribute the wheel, the violin, the printing press, and the cybernetic brain, to name a few of the inventions that have changed the course of history.

The IQ, a Comparative Score

Measuring your intelligence by means of an IQ test will give us your "intelligence quotient." Shall we return to *Webster's Third*?

> **Intelligence quotient**—a number held to express the relative intelligence of a person determined by dividing his mental age by his chronological age with chronological years above 14 and sometimes 16 disregarded and then multiplying by 100 to eliminate decimals.

So your IQ is a score, a number that tells us how *relatively* intelligent you are for your age compared with others in your age or societal group. The number is arrived at by means of an IQ test, sometimes the Stanford-Binet or the Wechsler Scale. Sometimes, but not always, because there have been numerous tests designed in an effort to yield up similar information. Although IQ tests were developed originally to evaluate children, there are far more complex tests available today for people of all ages.

The Development of the IQ Test

The Stanford-Binet, probably the most famous of the IQ tests and usually the one people think of when they use the term "IQ test," first saw the light of day in France in the year 1905. That was the same year that a twenty-six-year-old Swiss genius, Albert Einstein, revised Newtonian physics by publishing his paper on a baffling new theory, with its mysterious equation, $e = mc^2$, which he named the Theory of Relativity. If understanding the Theory of Relativity was a test of human intelligence, it was a test that 999 people out of 1,000 flunked.

In 1904, the Paris Ministry of Public Instruction, seeking to differentiate between slow learners and other children in order to determine the need for and to create budgets for special schools, commissioned Theodore Simon and Alfred Binet, who was the head of the Laboratory of Experimental Psychology at the Sorbonne, to devise a test that would evaluate the schoolchild by fixing a rate of learning that was "normal" for his mental age. The original test contained 54 areas, the first revision expanding that to 90, and the later revision to 129, with a dramatic increase in the amount of nonverbal testing in response to critics of the test who charged that verbal ability had been too heavily weighted in the original test.

The Simon-Binet became the Stanford-Binet in 1916 when it was first revised and expanded by Lewis Terman of Stanford University (as it was again in 1937 and once more in 1960). It set a series of intellectual standards for two-year-olds to twenty-three-year-old adults. The Stanford-Binet test includes such categories as reading comprehension, comparing similarities and contrasting opposites, vocabulary, memory, picture completion, and so on. A complete listing of the test categories is given later in this chapter.

The Stanford-Binet, through its revisions, which have made it broader and at the same time more accurate, has become a standard method for clinical evaluation of human intelligence levels, including "normal," gifted, and retarded, extending from early childhood into adulthood.

In 1949, the Wechsler Intelligence Scale for Children

22

was made standard by testing an extremely specific group of 2,200 children: They were all Caucasian, they all spoke English, and they all came from households where the fathers worked in one of nine specified fields. Obviously, in so limited a spectrum, a workable comparison could be made among children belonging to that group, but no truly valid conclusions could be drawn about children outside the testing parameters. In the intervening four decades, however, new Wechsler tests have been introduced so that a much broader base of people of different ages and social situations may be tested.

What the Wechsler (often called the WAIS, short for Wechsler Adult Intelligence Scale) does is to offer a series of tests, each category testing a different aspect of intelligence, such as knowledge of general information, ability to reason logically, to reason practically, visual comprehension, vocabulary, and more. The scope of the Wechsler test is broader than that of the Stanford-Binet, but both major IQ tests have been attacked by those who accuse the tests of being culturally biased in favor of the middle-class child, not objective enough, and based on learning rather than innate ability.

Two of these critics, a Canadian psychologist, Dr. John Ertl, and Dr. Bernard Elliot, a Canadian electrical engineer, point out that conventional IQ test scores for the same child vary greatly, sometimes by as much as twenty or thirty points, and are therefore unreliable. They have devised an entirely new way of testing the intelligence quotient, a test that asks no questions at all, neither written nor oral, a test that is unconcerned with what the subject has learned in school or out of it. All the testing subject has to do is look at a light.

Wearing electrodes on his or her skull that pick up brain waves, the person being tested is hooked up to a computer that amplifies the waves, shows them on an oscilloscope, and flashes a light every second for two minutes. The computer then records how quickly the eye—therefore the brain—responds to the light. That's all there is to the test, which Drs. Elliot and Ertl claim is entirely objective, and a true reading of the ability to learn.

Criticisms and flashing lights aside, how does a conventional IQ test actually work, and how valid are the results? Can an intelligence test measure anything other than our ability to handle that particular test? In the case of the best ones, probably. The specific questions correlate to the general standard of intelligence in a way that gives the professional tester a good idea of the capability of the person tested.

"Getting It": How an IQ Test Works

To give you an insight into how an intelligence test works, let us take a journey back in time, to Tuscumbia, Alabama. It is March, 1887, and we are standing near an ordinary water pump, waiting to witness one of the greatest dramatic moments in human endeavor, a moment often referred to as a "miracle."

We see a little girl of seven, blind, deaf, mute, locked away from the light of education and experience, but possessing a formidable, ferocious intelligence. Helen Keller was a normal, happy, bright baby, but at the age of nineteen months she was struck down by a mysterious ailment and a high fever that left her without sight or hearing.

An extraordinary teacher, Annie Sullivan, herself almost blind, has just come into the child's life to attempt to teach little Helen, who up to now has been judged virtually unreachable. For weeks, Sullivan has been spelling out the names of familiar common objects into little Helen's hand, using the deaf-mute alphabet. If she can only get the child to realize that her favorite doll or the cake she loves have names of their own, that they can be asked for by means of spelling out with fingers, that specific words have specific commonly agreed-upon meanings, and that these meanings do not change, so that words are the tools used in communication, the lock of little Helen's dark world will be opened.

D-O-L-L. C-A-K-E. Annie has spelled them over and over, and so far Helen has grasped only that if she makes the same finger movements, imitating Annie Sullivan like a little monkey, she will be given her doll or a piece of cake. What she has not grasped is the most important thing; she has not made the connection between the finger-spelling and the *name* of the object.

Annie and Helen have been working on the word "water." Again and again, Annie Sullivan has spelled out W-A-T-E-R into the palm of Helen's hand.

Let us watch what happens now, that miraculous moment when Annie Sullivan grasps Helen Keller's seven-year-old hand and thrusts it under the pump, allowing the cold water to flow onto it, and let us tell the story in Helen Keller's own words, taken from her autobiography, *The Story of My Life:*

> As the cool stream gushed over one hand, she spelled into the other the word water, first slowly, then rapidly. I stood still, my whole attention fixed upon the motion of her fingers. Suddenly I felt a misty consciousness as of something forgotten—a thrill of returning thought; and somehow the mystery of language was revealed to me. I knew then that W-A-T-E-R meant the wonderful cool something that was flowing over my hand. . . .

This, then, was the point at which Helen Keller's intelligence took over from her instincts, and Helen "got it." She made the crucial connection between the tappings into her hand and a word that spelled "water," the even more crucial connection between the word and the substance itself, and the quantum leap into the knowledge that this connection could happen over and over again.

What intelligence tests attempt to do is to gather representative samplings of the existing methods of "getting it" and to lay them out in the form of a test. The areas of testing, covering the existing methods of grasping basic principles, may be verbal, non-verbal, mathematical, concrete or abstract, learned or intuitive, as we shall see.

Measuring Intelligence Specifically

How is intelligence measured specifically? Let's use young Helen again as our example. Let us suppose that there were three Annie Sullivans, each with a different way of getting through to three blind and deaf Helens, but that Helen I only "got it" when Annie I pumped the cold water over her hand, while Helen II was able to "get it" through two methods, the water over her hand and her favorite cake, connecting the water with the word and connecting the aroma and taste of the cake with the spelling of C-A-K-E simultaneously on the palm of her hand. Helen III might grasp the principle that objects have names by means of three approaches by Annie III—the cold flowing water, the cake, and the emotional appeal of the beloved doll, D-O-L-L.

Helen III would test as the "most accessible," more intelligent than the other two, while Helen II is more intelligent than Helen I. Testing and verifying all the representative methods of understanding is a basic feature of a good IQ test. Also, between not understanding and understanding lie all the gradations of *how quickly* that comprehension was accomplished.

But there's yet another factor: age. Let us further suppose that Helen Keller had a twin, Ellen, also deaf and blind. Helen "got it" at the age of seven, making the crucial connection between objects and words, but Ellen doesn't "get it" until she is fifteen. The test presumption is, understandably, that Helen is brighter than Ellen. Comparing ages is another basic feature of good IQ tests. A subject's mental age refers to his mental age on a particular intelligence test. In actuality, we all have more than one mental age. Someone who tests badly may be a musical genius (Mozart might well have tested poorly in most areas) or have an awesome mechanical aptitude, for example. In those areas, his or her mental age would be well above that of chronological peers, although an individual might score well under his or her age group in a standard intelligence test.

What Helen Keller achieved at seven—the "miracle"—was insight, obviously divorced from most other stimuli and input because of the lack of sight and sound. Insight is a category on the Stanford-Binet test. Differentiating among methods of "getting it" is more subtle for people in full possession of all five senses, yet the intention of IQ tests is just that—to so differentiate.

Helen is more intelligent than her hypothetical twin sister Ellen. IQ tests not only identify that she *is* more intelligent, they attempt to quantify *how much* more. Loosely speaking, each individual section of the test is meant to represent another means of "getting it," making that crucial connection between problem and solution.

Taking the Stanford-Binet

The categories of the Stanford-Binet intelligence test for adults are:

Vocabulary	Repeating Digits Reversed
Codes	Sentence Building
Differences between Abstract Words	Essential Similarities
	Finding Reasons
Arithmetical Reasoning	Reconciliation of Opposites
Proverbs	Repeating Thought of Passage
Ingenuity	Orientation
Memory for Sentences	Opposite Analogies

Let's demonstrate right here what we mean. On the left-hand page are representative (but paraphrased) test questions from the various areas of a conventional intelligence test. On the right-hand page, corresponding to the questions, is the real meaning of the question—what part of your intelligence is actually being tested here.

Because I want you to give more thought to the question than to the answer itself, I'm going to give you a guideline for each question. Follow each guideline before answering the question. The purpose here is to show you in a very rough form how many ways to think you have available, how many ways of "getting it." Later, the Brain Builders and their accompanying exercises will go into this subject much more deeply and explicitly.

Ready? Go.

Form

1) *VOCABULARY:* What is a unicycle? ☞
(Guideline: Look up the word "unicycle" in your pocket dictionary. Now picture the unicycle in your mind and write down everything you know or have just learned about it.)

2) *OPPOSITE ANALOGIES:* A mirror is opaque; a window is _____? ☞
(Guideline: Look up the word "opaque." Think about the properties of opacity as you answer the question.)

3) *ARITHMETICAL REASONING:* If you saved $200 this month and spent half ☞
of that on a pair of tennis shoes and a sweatshirt, the shoes costing three times as much as the shirt, how much did the shirt cost?
(Guideline: Instead of dividing and multiplying numbers, draw a picture of the problem, using stacks of "money" labeled "savings," "shirt," "shoes," the stacks being in the same proportion as the costs in the problem. The answer is arrived at easily, but the important thing is that the *concept* of arithmetic becomes apparent.)

4) *INGENUITY:* If you have a three-pint container and a two-pint container, how ☞
can you measure out one pint?
(Guideline: Once again, draw your answer as a series of containers, each holding the amount called for in the problem. In other words, visualize the problem of answering it by rote arithmetic.)

5) *DIFFERENCES BETWEEN ABSTRACT WORDS:* What is the difference between ☞
being alone and being lonely?
(Guideline: Even though you think you already know the meaning of the words, look up "alone" and "lonely" in your dictionary. Compare the differences between them. Can you add to the list?)

6) *PROVERBS:* If it ain't broke, don't fix it. ☞
(Guideline: Consider the consequences—what could happen if you change something that is working well?)

7) *ESSENTIAL DIFFERENCES:* What is the difference between pleasure and pain? ☞
(Guideline: Once more, even though you think you are totally familiar with this pair of "opposites," look up both words—"pleasure" and "pain." Could there be anything of one in the other? Or are they mutually exclusive? Are they by definition opposites?)

Function

1) How well are you able to process successfully the wealth of information coming to you in the form of words?

2) Beyond receiving information, are you able to use it?

3) Are you able to use logic?

4) Are you able to create your own path in the jungle of the intellect?

5) Are you able to make distinctions between concepts?

6) Are you able to generalize from the particular?

7) Do you know how things get to be called opposites?

8) *RECONCILIATION OF OPPOSITES:* How are short and tall alike?   ☞
(Guideline: Consider the example of a short person and a tall person. Are "short" and "tall" absolute or relative concepts? Could any tall person be considered short in another society or measured against another person, say, Dr. J, the star basketball player?)

9) *ESSENTIAL SIMILARITIES:* What is the principal way in which fruits and   ☞
vegetables are alike?
(Guideline: Look up the definitions of "fruit" and "vegetable.")

10) *FINDING REASONS:* Give three reasons why we should have a government.   ☞
(Guideline: Think as quickly as possible of *ten* reasons. List a key word of each reason, even if they don't seem to be totally convincing. Then, select the three best.)

The preceding are some of the categories in which our intelligence is tested and assigned a number value, the intelligence quotient. You can project the questions on the right-hand page onto your own business and personal life and see how valid the categories are—dealing with information, distinguishing between concepts, generalizing from the particular, seeing how various opposing poles relate to one another—these areas are, basically, what living in the real world is all about.

This, too, is what Brain Building is all about. As you go on building your brain power with the Brain Builder exercises you will not only be adding to the number of ways in which you can think and reason, you will be adding to the ways in which you can control and direct your own life.

And, as if that goal is not inspiration enough, let's go back to that eminent contemporary philosopher Alfred North Whitehead and hear his words:

> Our minds are finite, and yet even in these circumstances of finitude we are surrounded by possibilities that are infinite, and the purpose of human life is to grasp as much as we can out of that infinitude.

8) In order to understand why things are at opposing ends of the pole, you need to be able to identify the pole itself. Can you?

9) And are you able to see how different poles relate to one another?

10) Beyond knowing the way things are, are you capable of understanding *why* they are the way they are?

Brief Quiz

ANOTHER SHORT UNWRITTEN QUIZ,
TO TAKE ON SATURDAY NIGHT

1) What flatworms were involved in a famous study of learning?
2) What if the "educated" flatworms were taught errors?
3) Then can you digest information and be *worse* off?
4) What is an "intelligence quotient"?
5) What are the names of the two most famous intelligence tests?
6) Who was the first philosopher mentioned in this chapter?
7) And who was the last one?
8) When looking words up in your dictionary, did you find that the definition in your head was enhanced?
9) When you answered question #6 under the category "Form" on page 28 ("If it ain't broke, don't fix it") did you also realize that changing something that is working well might make it work *better*?
10) Do you feel that you need the author's answers to verify your score on the test illustration contained in this chapter?

THE ANSWERS

1) Planaria.
2) Another flatworm would gobble up wrong information.
3) You bet.
4) A number that is held to express your intelligence relative to other people.
5) The Stanford-Binet and the Wechsler.
6) Heraclitus.
7) Alfred North Whitehead.
8) I hope so.
9) I hope so even more on this one.
10) Did you answer "yes?" Then you could use a little more confidence. Read on.

CHAPTER

4

WEEK ONE: SATURDAY NIGHT

Warming Up with George

"To the vast majority of mankind nothing is more agreeable than to escape the need for mental exertion. . . . To most people nothing is more troublesome than the effort of thinking."

—James Bryce,
Studies in History and Jurisprudence

As with any program of exercise, *Brain Power* is not for the lazy. If someone sees no need in his life for mental exertion, he's probably right. The kind of life he's leading doesn't require it. Couch potatoes don't have to think; they are quite happy to sit and watch life roll by like the newsreel of an event taking place somewhere else.

But it doesn't have to be difficult, either. Whenever you begin a program of exercise, you start slowly, with a warm-up stretching period. If you are going to subject unused muscles to unaccustomed stress, then you start with a minimum of 10 to 20 minutes' stretching. The same goes for building your brain power. Not that you haven't been using your brain, but you have been using it in an undeliberate, unconscious kind of way, without a lot of stretching and without demanding that it operate at full capacity. Up to now, you've been taking your mind for granted.

Now that you have completed the first week of the program by learning about your brain, your intelligence, and how it's tested, let's start out with a special kind of warm-up quiz.

This quiz will not test your intellectual fitness; instead, it's designed to reveal whether your mind is awake or asleep. Are you thinking for yourself, or have you put your brain on "automatic pilot," letting others do your thinking for you? There may be some surprises in here, but try to answer every question as honestly as you can. And take your time answering; treat every question—even if it doesn't sound like a serious one—with equal seriousness. Honesty and seriousness are crucial for this quiz.

I suggest that you take this quiz at night because most people's defenses are geared up in the morning and by evening have weakened somewhat. More secrets are told at midnight than at noon. (Not to mention that more things we'd like to keep secret are done at midnight than at noon.)

Because the automatic pilot on an aircraft is usually named George, I call this quiz:

George the Warm-Up

1. When you watch a funny movie at home, either on television or on your VCR, do you laugh out loud? Do you laugh as often or as hard as you do in a theater?

2. If you wear a size 8 shoe, would you decline to buy shoes marked size 6, even if they fit you perfectly?

3. When you lit up a cigarette for the first time or took your first alcoholic drink, were you alone or in the company of others?

4. Have you ever turned to your physician for nonmedical advice?

5. Do you like opera?

6. Can you tell if your favorite television or radio news program is liberal or conservative?

7. Do you still vote the same party as you did when you were eighteen?

8. Would you throw a fit if your government decided to take fifteen percent of all your personal belongings?

9. Do you have the same religion as your parents?

We told you there would be some surprises, didn't we? Here is how we score George, so get out your pencils:

1. If you laugh as hard at home as you do in a movie house, score 2. If not, score 0.

   This is a good example of the human tendency to put aside one's own thinking and accept the thinking of others. Common to all of us is the pressure to go along with the group, at least to some extent. Also, we feel more comfortable, safer in a group; our opinions aren't attributable to us, and we don't stand out. It's no accident that television sitcoms come complete with laugh tracks; people feel better about laughing out loud if they can hear others laughing, too. But sitcoms also come with "gasp" tracks and "awwww" tracks as well; your responses are being subjected to professional manipulation. What we may be timid about doing or saying as individuals, we will do or say in concert with others. However, this type of behavior has a numbing effect upon the intellect. It tends to validate and maintain whatever "groupthink" is current, whether or not it's accurate or true. Worse, it puts the mind out of the habit of thinking. People who let others direct their thinking eventually stop thinking for themselves entirely.
   Exercise: The next time you go out to see a movie, take note of how others react in the theater when they are surrounded by people. The next time you watch a film at home with a friend, give your companion no clue to your own reaction and watch his or her reaction.

2. If you would not buy the size 6 shoe, score 0 points. If you would, score 2.

   "If the shoes fits" is an example of many people's extreme reluctance to trust their own perceptions. Some of us have so little confidence in ourselves that we can be led away, even from the obviously correct. I once talked to an experienced shoe salesman who told me: "Many people have a size they consider 'their' size. If they see a shoe they like, and it doesn't fit them in 'their' size, they will not try on the next size up or down. They simply say 'The shoe doesn't fit,' and they walk out. In fact, even the people who do try on the next size don't buy as often as if 'their' size fit. And the further away from 'their' size they get, the less likely they are to buy." The shoe clerk added that, except in the case of children, whose size keeps changing, he has personally never sold a perfectly fitted shoe more than one full size away from the originally requested size!

3. If you were alone when you took your first drink or smoke, score 2; score 0 if you were in the company of others. If you have never taken a drink or a cigarette, score 0 if it's for religious reasons, score 2 if for other reasons.

There is just as much pressure upon you to conform as an adult as there was as an adolescent. If you were in the habit of giving in to pressure at an early age, there's a fair-to-good chance that you're still doing it. Old habits die hard, especially when the path they follow is the easier one. Women continue to wear clothing that is unflattering to them because fashion pressure dictates that they must follow the current styles. Men affect macho behavior that is not natural to them, in order not to be considered a wimp by others, even by others they don't respect.

4. Score 0 if you've asked your physician for nonmedical advice; score 2 if you haven't. If you know your physician socially, and you asked for the advice somewhere outside his office, score 2.

People tend to feel themselves intellectually inferior to anybody with a title, especially when the title is framed and hanging on the wall. In general, the less formally educated people are, the more they are impressed by the degrees, diplomas, and certificates of others. Those who feel themselves deeply inferior are often so overwhelmed that this awe extends even beyond the area covered by the title. More commonly, people simply don't question another's area of expertise if the expertise is backed by a bunch of framed degrees. Example: your plumber probably knows as much about pipes and welds as your doctor knows about bodies. But you wouldn't let your plumber march into your home and do anything he wanted to, would you? The chances are that you'd follow him around, watching him every step of the way. And if you felt his work wasn't good enough, you'd call another plumber without a moment's hesitation. But those same chances say you trust your doctor and wouldn't dream of second-guessing him. You're aware that plumbers vary in their competence; why shouldn't the same be true of physicians? Besides, your body is far more important to your well-being than your kitchen sink. So why do you trust your doctor so far out of proportion to his expertise? Could it be because he can write a title after his name?

Exercise: The next time you're talking to your doctor, tell him something he doesn't already know. Any fact will do (not medical, of course). The point is to overcome the idea that your physician is somehow on a higher intellectual plane than you just because he went to medical school.

5. Do you like opera? If you answered no: score 0 points if you've never seen one, 2 points if you have. If you answered yes: score 0 points if you've never seen one, 2 points if you have. The excuse "there is no opera house in my town" isn't good enough. Everyone has had many opportunities to see an opera on public television.

This question points up the almost automatic dislike of the unfamiliar and a reluctance to wander into unexplored intellectual territory. It's the adult version of a child's not wanting to eat anything green, of refusing even to taste it. If you scored 0 on this question, your reluctance is doing your mind great damage; you are wounding yourself intellectually. Opera itself, whether grand or light, is not the important thing here. Like it or dislike it as you please; that hardly matters. What is important is what "opera" symbolizes. It stands for the unfamiliar, and if you have an instinctive dislike and mistrust of the unfamiliar, you are in for a tough time in making intellectual progress. Don't tell yourself, "I don't have to be bitten by a snake to know I'm not going to like it." The analogy is a false one. People don't stand in line and pay out money to get bitten by a snake. They don't dress up in their Sunday best to be bitten by snakes. They don't shout "Bravo!" when the snake bites them. In fact, they don't deliberately arrange for snakes to bite them. (Except, perhaps, for Cleopatra.) On the other hand, if you said "yes" but have never seen one, then you are going along blindly with society's view that opera is culture, and you'd better agree or you will appear to be uncouth.

6. If you can tell whether your favorite news program is liberal or conservative, score 2 points. If you can't, it's a 0.

This is an example of believing what you want to believe. Newscasts, for the most part, are liberal or conservative in the same way that newspapers are. In all likelihood, your favorite newscast is mirroring your own views. That's why it's your favorite. If you honestly cannot tell what its bias is, you're not being objective. You're not "hearing" the slant because you really don't want to hear it; you'd prefer to go on thinking that the program, and you, are totally objective.

7. Do you vote the same way you did at eighteen? Score 0 if you do and have never had second thoughts about it. Score 2 if you've had second thoughts, whether or not you changed your vote.

The point made by this question is: do you or do you not benefit from experience? If you scored 0, you have refused to benefit and have caused severe harm to the growth potential of your intellect; you may even have impaired the intelligence of your behavior. If we all continue to vote as we did at eighteen, we would be a nation of political teenagers! Do you want this country to be governed by the wishes of its teenagers? "Older and wiser" may be a cliché, but it's a cliché that is rich with meaning. Politics and religion are generally the two most frequent examples of intellectual rigidity. Never again vote a straight party ticket by pulling one lever or punching out one hole. If you really want to vote your party down the line, at least do it by voting separately for each of your party's candidates, so that you're more aware of what you're doing.

8. If you would scream your head off should the government notify you that they are appropriating fifteen percent of your personal belongings, score 0. If not, score 2.

   What this question illustrates is how you can be intellectually conditioned. The U.S. government—through its arm, the Internal Revenue Service—is already taking at least that much; fifteen percent is the bottom line of the new tax laws. The money you earn is taxed before you can turn it into such personal possessions as clothing, furniture, appliances, a house, a car, a boat, jewelry, books, and so on. Therefore, you are already kissing fifteen percent of your personal possessions goodbye. But the U.S. didn't always have an income tax. Congress passed two other income tax bills—one in 1861 and one in 1894—but both were declared unconstitutional. The third bill, passed in 1913, stuck, and has been with us ever since. And you, having been born into the century of the income tax, have become so used to it that you accept it without question. The truly intellectual person "sees" things that others no longer see, if they ever did.

9. Do you have the same religion as your parents? Score 0 points if you do *and have never doubted or questioned its teachings*. Score 2 for any other answer.

   This is an example of dogmatism, the blind acceptance of received ideas. Religion itself is not the issue here; rather, its acceptance without question is the important matter. To adhere unflinchingly to childhood beliefs on any subject, to shut your mind to new ideas, or even to other old ideas, is death to the intellect. Besides, religions should have nothing to hide. They ought to *encourage* doubts and questions so that they can lay them to rest and reinforce faith.

Now it's time to add up your score on "George the Warm-up" and see whether your brain is on automatic pilot. We hope you have grasped our basic point—not to take the world around you for granted; it's filled with new ideas, wonderful new things to try. An open mind is your most important tool in building up your intelligence.

If you scored between 0 and 6, your brain is sound asleep, and you are spending so much time with George that you have allowed him to take over your intellect. You need to practice opening your eyes and your mind. Make that your first serious exercise. Start by asking questions about the most routine things in your life. Take nothing for granted, from your breakfast cereal to the newspaper you read. Question, question, question yourself until you begin to know why you do what you do. You're in for a few surprises.

If you scored between 6 and 12, you need work, but you're already well on your way to Brain Building. Go back over the questions on which you scored 0, and see which areas need the most stretching; concentrate on those. Become aware of the way in which your mind functions.

If you scored between 12 and 18, hooray for you! You've got what it takes to become a champion Brain Builder, an open and inquiring, doubting and questioning, fully functioning mind.

AND HERE'S A QUIZ ABOUT THE
QUIZ YOU'VE JUST TAKEN

1) What is the key to success of any exercise program?
2) What is the first step in Brain Building?
3) When you are at the movies, are your responses being quietly manipulated?
4) Would people smoke if they'd never seen anyone else smoke?
5) Is your doctor smarter than your lawyer?
6) Does virtually all news—written or broadcast—have a slant?
7) Why haven't you changed your political beliefs since college?
8) Does the federal government take your personal belongings?
9) Do your religious beliefs rely almost solely upon your parents rather than on reality?
10) Are most people on automatic pilot?

ANSWERS

1) Repetition.
2) Self-awareness.
3) Yes.
4) Probably not.
5) No. And you don't ask your *lawyer* about your personal life, do you? Then again, maybe you do!
6) Yes.
7) If you think that was an admonition, you're right!
8) Yes.
9) Yes.
10) Yes. And does the plane belong to their parents? And were *they* on automatic pilot *themselves*?

CHAPTER

5

WEEK TWO

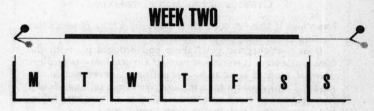

| M | T | W | T | F | S | S |

Building Vocabulary

TOOLS YOU WILL NEED FOR WEEK TWO:
A sharpened pencil *with an eraser* that is kept close to your
copy of *Brain Power* until you finish this book; a daily
newspaper; the dictionary you've been using up to now; some
money to buy a few books and magazines.

"Without knowing the force of words, it is impossible to know
men."

—Confucius

We'll start this chapter right out with the first of our Brain
Builders. Like the other Brain Builder exercises and challenges you'll encounter in this book, it is valid not only for
this chapter and this book, but may be used in areas of your
everyday life.

OVERCOME INTELLECTUAL TIMIDITY.

Exercise: If this is your own copy of *Brain Power*, start writing in the margins immediately.

Does that surprise you? Were you brought up with the idea that a book is somehow sacred? Do you feel—regardless of what kind of book it is—an obligatory reverence for its pages? Think about it for a minute. We're not talking about a fine art book or some rare first edition or a Gutenberg Bible, but an ordinary book that is mass-produced.

Reading an informational book should not be a passive act, with the author instructing while the reader is meekly instructed. Your own ideas are worthy, so record them. When you write your thoughts, reactions, comments, agreements and disagreements directly into a book, you already have an interactive dialogue going with the author. Sure, you could buy yourself a notebook, and leave the book's pages clean, but then there you'd be, back in school again, the author as teacher, the reader as student, while the book remains sacrosanct. The independence of your intelligence will benefit from your active participation.

Write in this book. We have provided you with extra-wide margins for your comments, so use them. Start right away; it will become easier to do when you've done it two or three times. The idea behind Brain Builder #1 is to help free you from an old hangup that has been interfering with part of your intellectual functioning.

BRAIN BUILDER #2

KEEP AN INTELLECTUAL "FIRST AID KIT"
AROUND THE HOUSE.

As you work through the pages of *Brain Power*, you will be putting your kit to more and better use. The kit should contain a good dictionary, unabridged if you can afford it, a thesaurus, an atlas, and a set of encyclopedias. Aside from the atlas, these may be purchased secondhand. It's always best to buy the most up-to-date books available, but if you can't afford to do that, an excellent source for low-cost versions of your "first aid kit" is the used-books counter at your local college bookstore or in student bookstores near the campus.

The dictionary should be a large one, not a pocket edition or a student edition; it should lie open well on a flat surface and have an easy-to-use pronunciation guide printed on every page; never, ever buy a dictionary with print so small you need a magnifying glass to read it!

The thesaurus must be unabridged; *Roget's* original format is still the best one available. Don't buy a thesaurus in dictionary form or one that is cluttered with extra material such as a listing of antonyms.

The set of encyclopedias may be up to five years old, provided it comes with a complete set of yearbook supplements bringing it up to date. You might even consider investing in *two* different old sets, especially if you can find them cheap (garage and yard sales often have encyclopedias for sale) and, whenever you look something up, read about it in both versions. You'll find the subject much easier to understand.

The atlas has to be brand-new, the most recent one available, and you should be prepared to replace it as soon as it becomes outdated, so perhaps a paperback atlas would be best. Buy the one easiest to use and with the largest index. Again, try to buy the best available, if you can. Your mind is more important than anything else you own.

Exercise: Make use of these books every day. Don't shelve them! These are tools for daily work, so they should be readily accessible. Keep them close at hand, waiting for you in a convenient spot. The dictionary, if possible, ought to lie open on a table; it's better for the spine (the book's, not yours) and the binding, and it looks (and is) inviting to browse through or pore over. Let your reference books become a part of your surroundings, like the lamp you switch on when it's dark. Every time you use them, you'll be switching on a light in your mind.

You say you don't have the spare cash to buy the "first aid kit" of reference books? How about selling something you already have but don't need? A second television set would be a great thing to get rid of.

Word Power

Let us begin building your brain power with words. Do you know the definition of "baleful" or "enormity" or "hang-dog"? How about "halcyon" or "fulsome"? What do the words "pagan" and "heathen" have in common? What is "livid" or "mundane"?

EXERCISE

Look up all nine words within quotation marks from the paragraph above—even if you think you know their meaning—in your good dictionary and score 1 point for each one you've correctly defined. Not as many as you thought, right? A great score is 6 and above; average is less than 3. If you have scored 0, don't be surprised; you've got a lot of company. But you've also got work to do.

Aside from "enormity," which runs to four syllables, most of our exercise words are no more than two syllables and can hardly be described as "long words." They're not even particularly difficult words, used (and mis-used) as they are in everyday speech. Yet many people get most of them wrong.

A well-developed vocabulary is the outward sign of a well-developed mind. Words are the working tools of your brain, just as surely as your hands or your eyes. We're very lucky, in that the English language, with its mixed legacy of nouns and verbs from Greek, Latin, and Anglo-Saxon (with its own Norse and Germanic heritage), is particularly rich. We have a definite name for nearly everything and a word for nearly every situation. Because of the rapid changes in American society and customs, new words are constantly entering the language—"shortfall," "countdown," "video." We have acquired words from every nationality that has come to our shores—"kibitz," "pizza," "croissant," "cabana"—to name only four out of thousands.

English is the language of Shakespeare, of Chaucer, Dickens, Henry James, Jane Austen, Virginia Woolf, John Donne and John Dryden, of Keats, Shelley, and Byron, of Samuel Johnson and Agatha Christie, of T.S. Eliot and Wallace Stevens, of Philip Roth and Mary Gordon, of Willa Cather and Sylvia Plath and Marianne Moore, of Russell Baker and James Michener, William Faulkner, F. Scott Fitzgerald, Ernest Hemingway and Katherine Anne Porter. Not making an effort to master the bountiful English language is like electing to stay hungry when a delicious feast is spread before you.

Words are the means by which you can express your thoughts. With precision of language, thoughts gain clarity as well as ease of expression, and communication with others improves. Long words are not better than short words; it's ideas that are important.

BRAIN BUILDER #3

LEARN TO UNDERSTAND YOUR LANGUAGE.

Exercise: Look up one word in common usage every day. As you are reading your daily newspaper, select one word to look up in the dictionary, even if you think you already know its definition. It can be a common word, one that you've used many times. But it should be a word about whose precise meaning you've always been curious or wanted to know more. If you can't get to a dictionary immediately, put the scrap of newsprint in your pocket or handbag, and don't forget to look the word up later the same day. Don't write the word into a notebook or even try to memorize it. Just read the definition, twice if necessary, without making a chore of it. Do this every day without fail; let the use of your dictionary become as comfortable and automatic as the use of your toothbrush.

BRAIN BUILDER #4

LEARN YOUR LANGUAGE.

Exercise: Every day, choose one word, one you're not sure you know, and look it up in the dictionary. Say the word out loud several times until you are at ease with its sound and its cadence. Don't go for the pompous, polysyllabic showoffs; simple language is usually the clearest. And don't study obscure words. You'll hardly ever use them, and if you do, your listeners will hardly ever understand them.

Go for the useful words, words that describe objects, actions, and even abstract ideas in the most precise way. Do this every day, but add the word to your speaking vocabulary casually, only if and when you please. Don't make a chore of it and don't spring it on others like a trap. No matter how quickly your vocabulary grows, never use a long word or an obscure one merely to impress your listener. Attempts to impress arise out of a lack of confidence, and they'll make you appear *less* intelligent than you are, not more.

Exercise: Learn to pronounce a new word daily. Every day, look up a word you come across in your daily reading but are unsure of how to pronounce. Say the word out loud correctly several times.

These are words you may be reluctant to use, even though you know their meanings, because you aren't sure how they are pronounced. Sometimes you hear respected figures, such as newscasters or politicians, pronounce them differently, and you assume that you must be the one who's wrong. Never assume that. Every day, media people massacre the English language publicly and others, convinced they can do no wrong, copy them without question. President Dwight D. Eisenhower used to say "nuke-you-lar" for "nuclear" (nu-klee-ar) and "Feb-you-ary" for "Feb-roo-ary," and he was not the only authoritative figure ever to mispronounce a word. We have been given what George Bernard Shaw described as "the divine gift of articulate speech," but we often misuse it.

A caution: Be careful not to take the pronunciation of many common words for granted. For starters, how do you pronounce the word "education"? Look it up as your word for today. The correct pronunciation may surprise you.

Exercise: Start listening for mispronunciations—in conversation, on the radio and television news, by leading figures, by yourself.

When you become a little more attentive to words in general and how to use them, you may begin to notice that others are making many errors. With continued attention, you may even see that you can count *yourself* among them. People, including you, are mispronouncing common, everyday words, and these people look bad to others who know the correct pronunciation of them. And don't make the mistake of thinking that the words you mispronounce aren't important ones, or that others are snobs for looking down on you because of it. "Mend your speech a little, lest you may mar your fortunes," wrote William Shakespeare, with good reason.

BRAIN BUILDER #5

AS YOUR MOTIVATION INCREASES,
ADD VOCABULARY BOOKS TO YOUR "FIRST AID KIT."

Exercise: Choose a vocabulary book that specializes in vocabulary-building through the use of the roots, or origins, of words. Once a week, learn the root of a familiar word.

Knowing roots opens up entire categories of words to you almost without effort. You'll learn not only the "what" of words, but the "why" and "when." The feeling you'll get might be something like going to a gym and seeing your chest expand or your waist contract by several inches in the first couple of weeks. Not surprisingly, it gets tougher after that, but then you'll have the moral support of your new measurements.

Do you think I'm making too much of correct pronunciation? How about this: Someone says to you, "I *slepp* so *late* this morning." He sounds fuzzyheaded and slovenly, a perpetual late riser. But someone who says crisply "I *slept* so *late* this morning" sounds as though sleeping late is a novelty for him.

Pronunciation is "a detail that makes all the difference." It says a great deal about people. If you do something so simple as to routinely wear the back end of your necktie three inches longer than the front, rather than the other way around, you must expect that people will notice that detail with disdain. So it is with faulty pronunciation; it stamps you as someone who isn't aware or doesn't care.

BRAIN BUILDER #6

INCREASE YOUR VOCABULARY PAINLESSLY IN THE BEGINNING.

Exercise: Start looking up words in specific subjects that you *like*, such as flowers, wine, cheese, or modern art. That way, you will easily expand your capacity to look for it, find it, buy it, eat it, drink it, and talk about it with some confidence. Choose a style of painting that appeals to you— for example "Impressionism," "Fauvism," or "Cubism." Look up the name of that style in the dictionary and see if it really means what you thought it did. Continue, using other words within the same context.

BRAIN BUILDER #7

ENLARGE YOUR SPECIFIC VOCABULARY'S SCOPE.

Exercise: Treat yourself to a subscription to a general magazine on a specific topic. But make it a topic that appeals to you, rather than one you feel you "should" know more about. There are too many "shoulds" in life. Choose a subject that interests you; visit the periodicals room of your local library, select a magazine that fulfills that interest, and subscribe to it. The most important thing about the new magazine is that you must read it when it drops through your mailbox. If it's going to lie languishing in the pile on your coffee table or beside your bed, save your money. It's also important that it not be too technical or written in a specialized language that causes you problems in understanding. But there will be words with which you are not familiar. Allow your own true interest and curiosity to increase your vocabulary naturally.

BRAIN BUILDER #8

INCREASE YOUR GENERAL VOCABULARY'S SCOPE.

Exercise: Read about topics of general interest. Subscribe to a relevant high-quality magazine of a broader scope and read it as soon as it arrives.

The important thing to remember is not to try too hard to learn and not to let yourself despair at what might seem to you to be a monumental task. Instead, just relax: enjoyment is the key here. Take the unfamiliar words as they occur in context and look them up occasionally. You'll remember the ones that hold most meaning for you; the others are far less important.

Here are a few suggestions for magazines that are worthwhile and will hold your attention. Are you interested in:

Literature?	*The Atlantic*
Geography?	*The National Geographic*
City life?	*The New Yorker*
Science?	*Scientific American*

UPGRADE YOUR VOCABULARY.

Exercise: In all of your reading, start reading newspapers, magazines, and books that are harder and more challenging than the ones to which you're accustomed. Don't make an effort to look up every single word you don't know. In fact, make an effort *not* to do this. Be selective. There are words you ought to be able to understand from context, if not the first time you see them used, then by the second, third, or fourth times. Every time you see such words thereafter, their definition will continue to be honed. Learning shouldn't be a chore; if you let it happen naturally, it will become a pleasure.

STOP USING SLANG.

If language is the coin of the intelligence by which we purchase ideas from one another, then slang must surely be the pennies. Give it up, especially those words used to describe other people negatively. Words like "ditz," "bimbo," "flake," "space cadet," and others like them are abominations. They actually put a stop to thinking by making final judgments about other people—judgments you won't re-examine. If you are accustomed to using slang, giving it up will be difficult, especially at first, but it will do wonders for your vocabulary.

Slang words merely take the place of more accurately descriptive words, and if you don't allow them into your everyday speech, you'll *have* to come up with the real words to say what you mean. And, to appeal to your vanity, nothing dates you like the slang you use. Imagine somebody you know using expressions like "hotcha," or "you dig?" You know exactly what decade he's frozen into, don't you? It takes a lot of time and effort to keep up with current slang, and if you have the leisure time to make that effort, why on earth waste it on slang?

Exercise: Listen to yourself speak, listen hard, and listen objectively. When you catch yourself using some current bit of jargon or slang, stop yourself, even if you've said the word already, and restate your sentence, using an appropriate non-slang expression. What *should* you have said instead? Say it now.

BRAIN BUILDER #11

STOP USING CLICHÉS.

"Hustle and bustle," "a hive of activity," "once in a lifetime" —there are thousands of expressions like these that are tired shortcuts around good vocabulary, taking the place of sharper, more original, more intelligent speech. Since words are the building blocks of thought, avoiding clichés in speech will force you to avoid them in thinking.

Exercise: Just as with slang, listen to yourself speak and catch the clichés. For each cliché you find yourself using, think of *two* colorful substitutes. What *should* you have said instead? Say it now.

BRAIN BUILDER #12

UPGRADE YOUR "PERSONAL" VOCABULARY.

Exercise: Don't hesitate to ask somebody the meaning of a word he or she has just used. Listen carefully to the words as well as the substance of what's being said to you. Don't interrupt the other person, but make a mental note of the word, and ask the question as soon as the speaker has finished.

Although not every situation is ideal for asking—you don't always want to stop the flow of narrative, for example—there are many times when it's perfectly comfortable and acceptable to ask. People are flattered at being asked to explain, and it shows you're listening carefully. Even if the definition offered isn't perfect, it's probably more than you knew before. The beginning of wisdom, as the wise man said, is to know that you do not know.

BRAIN BUILDER #13

CONSIDER THE STUDY OF LATIN INFLUENCES
ON THE ENGLISH LANGUAGE.

Exercise: Read the section about Latin as a language in your encyclopedia to get some understanding about the subject. Latin is far from a dead language; it's the living repository of so many English roots that a study of it will greatly enhance your understanding of vocabulary. Catholic colleges or universities often offer Latin classes in the evening and admit nonmatriculating students.

If you do sign up for Latin, take the course that emphasizes Latin influences on the English language and Roman history as part of the course of study. This is supposed to be fun for you, not a "return to school." Ideally, you should simply audit the course, without taking it for credit and without exams.

Don't Let Words Remain Strangers

Remember that your ideas are only as clear as the words that express them. Don't keep words at arm's length as strangers; let them approach and become your friends and even your servants. Think of Helen Keller; it was a single word, "water," that started her on the path from silent darkness to the light of a useful life and world acclaim.

If you have followed your list of Brain Builders faithfully, you will have added a minimum of 15 usable word-tools to your vocabulary in the first week alone. Do you know the most important thing about these words?

You chose them yourself.

You have selected and made your own a group of words relevant to yourself and your interests, to the way you live, and to the things you are curious about. They weren't presented to you in an alphabetical listing of words you "ought" to know; instead, they became yours in the most natural way possible, to be of the greatest possible usefulness.

A Short Quiz for the End of Week Two

1) Why should the dictionary be a large one?
2) Which thesaurus should you get?
3) Why can the encyclopedias be a few years old?
4) Why does the atlas have to be new?
5) Why shouldn't you study obscure words?
6) Why should you study the roots of words?
7) Why should you stop using slang?
8) Why should you stop using clichés?
9) Why should you study anything that has to do with Latin?
10) Why should you increase your vocabulary?

Answers

1) So it'll have more words!
2) *Roget's* in the original format only.
3) Because very little is going on in ancient Greece and ancient Rome these days. In other words, most of the information in the encyclopedia is old anyway, but the yearbooks help keep it up to date.
4) Because political information changes constantly.
5) Because you won't use them, and others won't understand them.
6) It's a time-saving and effort-saving study tool.
7) Because it makes you think like a conformist.
8) Because they make you think like a conformist.
9) Because it will help you to understand English.
10) For the same reason that a three-year-old should increase it!

CHAPTER

6

WEEK THREE

M T W T F S S

Building a Calculating Brain

TOOLS YOU WILL NEED FOR WEEK THREE:
A metric ruler; a Celsius thermometer; a small hand-held
calculator.

"Mathematics is the science which draws necessary conclusions."

—Benjamin Pierce, in the *American
Journal of Mathematics, vol. IV [1881]*

Now that you're well into *Brain Power*, I must confess
that this section is going to deal with—among other things—
mathematics. I kept the word "mathematics" out of the
chapter title because, frankly, those four syllables strike
terror into the hearts of many intelligent people. When you
picked up this book for the first time, you may have skimmed
the table of contents, and I didn't want that eleven-letter

word leaping out at you, sending you screaming into the streets.

Take heart. You'll be looking at math in a whole new way, a way you can easily grasp.

Exercise: Have you written in the margins of this book yet? If not, why not? Brain Builder #1 will help unstifle your intelligence, taking one area at a time. Objective thinking is the most important function of your intellect. Can you add anything to the thought? Write it down in this book. If ink still intimidates you, write it in pencil if you must, but do it!

Let's Plunge Right In

EXERCISE

Try this quickly, without stopping to puzzle it out, and without pencil and paper. What is 12 divided by ½? If you give the answer as 6, if you are facing a chapter about mathematics with a sinking heart and a queasy feeling in your insides, if you have said all your life "math is/was my poorest subject," welcome to the club and take courage. The fear and loathing of mathematics is so common that it could be called the rule rather than the exception. (The correct answer is 24.)

Even the great English philosopher and mathematician Alfred North Whitehead acknowledged the difficulties of the subject:

> The study of mathematics is apt to commence in disappointment. . . . We are told that by its aid the stars are weighed and the billions of molecules in a drop of water are counted. Yet, like the ghost of Hamlet's father, this great science eludes the efforts of our mental weapons to grasp it.
> —Alfred North Whitehead, *An Introduction to Mathematics*, 1911

Be consoled by the fact that a grasp of mathematics has less to do with your intelligence than your education. If you don't understand the basic principles of math, you were probably badly taught somewhere along the way. The problem with many people is that after they get past the age at which they *should* have learned something, they become embarrassed if they haven't and therefore back away from anything and everything involved with it. They feel that they've been left too far behind and that catching up is too big a task.

You're Not a Mathematical Misfit

Believe me, you're not the mathematical misfit you may think you are. After all, you function in the real world. Somehow you manage to hold a job, balance a checkbook, use credit cards, pay taxes. If you think you can't forge ahead from the simple arithmetic required in these daily operations think again. Math has suffered a bum rap all these years. Mathematical thinking is easier than you supposed. It can even be fun.

"Yes, but," I can hear you asking, "if I can get through life exactly as I do—paying bills and taxes, balancing my checkbook, doing well at my job—without dealing with the principles of mathematics, why should I come to grips with it now? Why should I trouble my brain with this stuff when a ten-dollar calculator does it all for me—and faster?"

The answer is simple: familiarity with mathematics will expand your power, make your intellect stronger, and be of immense help in using logic, which is itself of immense help in life. But there are even more compelling reasons. Mathematics is, after all, a system of conceptual control that allows us to operate more efficiently. In this way, it's much like the notion of time. It allows us to capture an idea, manipulate it for our own purposes, experiment with it, describe it within given parameters, and use it for many important and not-so-important functions.

Mathematics Is Something We All Agree Upon

Also, like language, mathematics is something *agreed-upon* in communication. We all know what is meant by the words "I'm cold." We have agreed upon the definition of "cold" and can communicate its meaning to one another. Similarly, people have agreed upon numbers. If I say to you, "There are three apples on this table," you know exactly what I mean by "three." And numbers are far more precise than language is. "Cold" to you and me might mean 50 degrees Fahrenheit while to an Eskimo it might mean −10 degrees and to the Kalahari bushman it might mean a balmy 70. We may be forced to refine the definition of "cold" further to communicate better. But not so with numbers. Whether in the U.S. or the U.S.S.R., whether on Earth or on Mars, 3 is 3. As Lancelot Hogben says in his excellent book, *Mathematics for the Million,* a book I urge you to add to your intellectual first aid kit, "The language of Mathematics differs from everyday life, because it is essentially a rationally planned language." It is that quality of rationality to which this chapter is dedicated.

Mathematics Is a Useful Tool

Mathematics allows you to extend your intellectual reach; in that way it's similar to the pole a maintenance man uses to unscrew a ceiling light bulb that's out of his reach. It's a tool, there for you to use once you've learned to use it.

On one hand, numbers are absolute and authoritative. They don't give an inch. An answer is either right or wrong; there is no shade of gray ("Well, maybe . . .") in mathematics. This absolutism terrifies many people and turns them off.

But just take a look at the flip side. Numbers are predictable and comforting. They don't sneak up on you as words sometimes do. In mathematics, you don't have anything tricky to deal with—like "cough," "enough," and "bough," for example, all of which have identical endings that are pronounced differently; or "seen" and "scene" or "discreet" and "discrete," which are pronounced alike but have different meanings.

Exercise: If you aren't certain of the meaning of "discrete," go and look it up now. (Its definition is probably not at all what you thought it was.)

You Can Count on Numbers

But numbers are not that way. The significance of the number 5 never varies; no matter where it appears in the equation, 5 is always 5. It behaves like 5 in any mathematical situation, never 4 or 6. There are few things in the world as constant, as unvarying, and as reliable as numbers.

This is one of the reasons mathematics will serve you extremely well in your day-to-day life, in your home, in your workplace, and in the many areas of intellectual thought you may be exploring. You can trust math. Numbers are friends that are unchanging in their loyalty to the intellect.

Here's a little six-minute, four-problem mini-test to determine if you possess a mathematical mind. You'll find the answers at the end of this chapter.

PROBLEM I (SOLUTION TIME: 1 MINUTE)

Given: 2 stars + 1 moon = 10; 1 moon + 1 sun + 1 star = 9; 1 star + 2 moons = 8; 1 star + 1 flower + 1 sun = 12. Find the numerical value of each symbol.

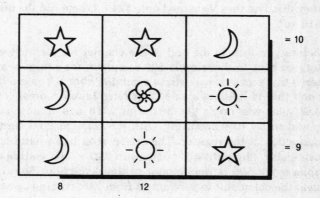

PROBLEM II (SOLUTION TIME: 2 MINUTES)

Three men decide to share a hotel room for reasons of economy. The desk clerk tells them the room costs $30, and each puts up $10. Later, the clerk realizes that he has made a mistake. The room rate is $25, not $30. He gives the bellman $5 and tells him to return it to the three men. The bellman, however, doesn't know how to divide $5 among three men, and so he gives $1 to each of them and keeps $2 for charity. The men have now paid $9 each for the room, and $9 × 3 = $27; the bellhop has $2, and that makes $29. What happened to the other dollar?

PROBLEM III (SOLUTION TIME: 3 MINUTES)

Two men are selling neckties; one sells them at the price of 2 for $10, the other at the price of 3 for $10. They decide to merge instead of competing, and each man contributes 30 neckties so that they have a common stock of 60 neckties; they will sell these at 5 ties for $20. Why not? After all, doesn't "3 for $10" plus "2 for $10" add up to "5 for $20"? If the first man had sold all 30 of his ties separately, at 2 for $10, he would have earned $150; if the second man had sold all of his at 3 for $10, he would have earned $100. Added together, they would have earned $250 for 60 ties. Instead, when they've sold them all jointly, they discover they've earned only $240. Where did the other $10 go?

Before you turn to the end of the chapter for the answers, let's go back to that simple $20 calculator for a minute and see if this scene doesn't strike a familiar chord. You are in a shop that is holding a sale. You have found a dress (or a suit) that was originally priced at $240 and is now supposed to be 40 percent off, with the salesclerk taking the deduction at the register. The salesperson has a hand-held calculator. She dutifully punches in 240 × .40, getting the answer 96; $96 is the amount of the deduction. She then uses the calculator to subtract 96 from 240, coming up with the correct sale price of $144.

Is anything wrong with that?

Yes. If the clerk had the most basic knowledge of percentages, she would know that the baseline figure where percentages are concerned is 100. Actually, she probably *does* know it but is reluctant to "experiment" with expanding the concept because it's "math." If the reduction is 40 percent off the price of 100 percent ($240) the customer must therefore pay 60 percent. (If the sale price is 30 percent less, the shopper pays 70 percent; if half-price, the shopper pays 50 percent, and so on.) If the clerk took the $240 figure and multiplied it by .60, the answer would still be $144, but it would have been arrived at in one operation of the calculator, not two.

The salesclerk is making her own life more difficult. She cannot get out of a calculator what she hasn't put into it, which in this case is the capability to approach the problem logically, to achieve the correct answer in the fewest possible steps.

Two things are operating here: although saving a little bit of time is not the point, a few seconds lost in every sales transaction she figures twice with her calculator can add up to a significant chunk of time, especially on a busy day—when the store runs an ad, for example, or when it holds its seasonal clearances. Also, she's likely to double her error rate.

When you understand how numbers function with mathematical precision, you'll save anything from little bits of time to huge blocks of time. It helps a person to make choices based on reality and logic rather than on guesswork. Then, too, our salesclerk simply isn't doing her job as efficiently as she might. Being unable to handle little concepts deftly could make her unable to handle greater concepts deftly or at all. Larger concepts are the ones that make great differences in a salesclerk's life—and yours.

For example, these range from how you spend your time—maximizing either your leisure time or your earning capacity—to whether you decide to take a different job in another city. A mathematically logical point of view helps you to take into account all possible factors and weigh them unemotionally according to their relative significance *before* adding in the emotional factors. Thinking mathematically will help you separate emotion and intellect; confusing the two is absolute anathema to powerful intellectual functioning.

There's nothing wrong with taking emotional factors into account as long as you recognize them for what they are—feelings and not facts. A sound mathematical mind will help you discover which facts truly impact on any given situation and which have nothing to do with it.

EXERCISE

Using your hand-held calculator, see approximately how much time in your life you will lose if you waste five minutes each day through being poor at mathematics. Let's assume that you will live until the age of 80, and that you begin your calculation at the age of 10.

Let's take another simple example. Banks and other lending institutions offer credit cards; "grace periods" and the percentage of interest charged on the unpaid balances vary, sometimes greatly. If you are like so many other Americans, you carry more than one type of credit card. You may be using credit cards that charge you 14 percent annually or as much as 19.8, cards that grant you as little as 5 days' time in which you aren't charged a finance charge to as much as 25 days.

EXERCISE

Do you know which credit cards you use charge the lowest interest? The highest? Which of them gives you the most generous grace period to pay your bills? Find out now. If you carry only one card, are you paying the lowest rate available in the United States? If not, why not? Do you have a good reason?

Interest rates and grace periods are required by law to be printed on every monthly statement, even though they're usually buried somewhere in the fine print on the bottom or on the back. A distaste for dealing with numbers might cause you to overlook this valuable information. Why should you pay extra interest? Where's the logic in it?

Or maybe you use your mathematical thinking to come up with another conclusion entirely: you don't care. Sure, you don't want to spend money on finance charges unnecessarily, but you've calculated how much time you'd have to spend to chase after those dollars, and you've decided it isn't worth it. You've concluded, after working it out, that it will actually cost you money in lost earning-power time if you try to plug all the holes through which your money is seeping. To many people, this kind of thinking makes sense; it's applicable to their own situations, and it's just as valid a use to which you can put mathematics as is the calculation of all the ways you can hang onto your money.

This is, actually, one of the most important points I make in this chapter. You need to stop seeing mathematical ability as only applying to the kind of things you learned in grade school and high school. Those long-ago problems—of how many apples and oranges can Susie buy and how long will it take the frog to get out of the well if it hops two steps forward and one back—were the most elementary uses to which mathematics can be put. Far more sophisticated uses are the higher mathematics used in the sciences and the higher forms of mathematical reasoning used in areas of thought not commonly perceived to be mathematical at all.

For example, the strongest diagnostic attack on a medical problem will be almost purely mathematical, including not only factors that currently can be quantified, that is, made numerical, but also factors that must be included mathematically, whether those factors are quantifiable or not. Sometimes, mathematical reasoning may be exhausted because our current state of knowledge in a specific area lacks key elements. Even so, reasoning will be used as far as we can take it on the theory that an educated guess is still far better than an uneducated one.

APPROACH MATHEMATICS FROM A NEW DIRECTION.

Exercise: Take a simple math problem in arithmetic—addition, subtraction, multiplication, and/or division, and draw a picture of it.

When a rock star picks up his guitar and strikes a chord, he never stops to think that the sound produced is the direct result of numerical ratios as detailed by Pythagoras. But as a musician, he does know, even without being taught, that there's a logical pattern behind the E chord or the G chord—their transitions and intervals—a logic that doesn't vary. Begin to see mathematical reasoning in terms of logical reasoning. After all, that's exactly what it is: mathematical reasoning is merely logical reasoning that is quantifiable, that is, reasoning to which numbers can be attached. As a demonstration of that principle, why not try drawing a picture? For example, let's suppose that in England there's a town called Smither in the county of Splint. A simple picture of it would look like this:

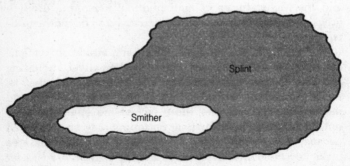

When you look at the drawing, you can tell easily that all Smithereens are Splinters, but not all Splinters are Smithereens. But if we had told you beforehand that this simple drawing would symbolize a diagrammed mathematic set and subset, and that from it a logical inference could be made, you might have knocked over your chair trying to get away. Yet the drawing is simplicity itself, totally understandable, and the solution was painless.

Don't allow the miserable manner in which you were taught mathematics in grade school and high school turn you off to this enormously powerful intellectual tool that can increase your mental power in nearly every aspect of your life.

Let's try another example with another set of drawings. But first, let me state the problem in arithmetical terms. Just read it through without making an effort to solve it:

You earned $52,000 last year. One quarter of it went to taxes. The rest appreciated by a third, thanks to a wildly profitable investment. However, after you told your friends about the stock, one of them talked you into lending him half your money, and he never paid you back. To avoid sinking into depression, you treated yourself to a down payment on a dark blue Mercedes with half the money you had left. How much do you have now?

If you recognize the above as your old friend the sixth-grade math problem—how many apples and oranges can Susie buy, only updated to the fast lane of the 1980s—it is. But we are going to understand it in an entirely new way, with simple drawings.

You earned $52,000 last year. A quarter of it went to taxes.

$ 13,000	$ 13,000	$ 13,000	

$52,000

The rest appreciated by a third, thanks to a lucky investment.

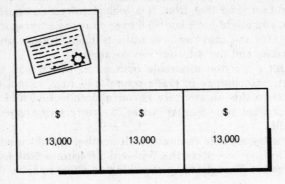

After you told a friend, he borrowed half your money, and you can kiss it goodbye forever.

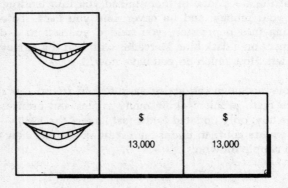

To avoid depression, you laid out half of what you had left as a down payment on the Mercedes of your dreams.

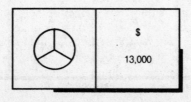

How much do you have now?

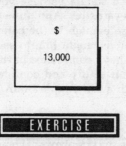

$
13,000

EXERCISE

Try the following problem using the same method of drawing pictures that I showed you in the last solution.

PROBLEM IV

You earned $63,000 last year. One-third of it went to your ex-wife, whom you divorced when you discovered that she married you for your money. The rest appreciated by one-half when you sold your Porsche to make ends meet. Then you lent your new girlfriend two-thirds of that. Of the remaining amount, the government took an additional two-thirds. Have you any money and/or sanity left? How much? (Money, that is. You obviously didn't *start* with enough sanity.)

Don't Worry About Crossing Those "T"'s

Don't be afraid of thinking with mathematical logic. In other areas of your life you think subjectively, and you're much less afraid of making an error. What if you aren't exactly correct down to the last detail? It's the overall rightness that counts, not the dotting of the "i" and the crossing of the "t." The quality of your daily life doesn't depend on perfect objective decisions any more than it does on perfect subjective decisions. Try thinking about math in the same way. Before you turn to your calculator or even to pencil and paper, make an educated guess.

Let's presume you're having new carpeting put down in your home. You've telephoned several carpet companies to come in and give you estimates. Nine times out of ten, the more experienced carpet-measurer can look around and tell you how much square yardage you'll need before he even pulls out his yardstick. And, nine times out of ten, his guess will be close enough to the carefully-measured distance. Experience has taught him to *see* "how much," and he has learned to have confidence in that ability.

You too can gain ability and confidence in your ability in those areas with a few simple Brain Builders.

BRAIN BUILDER #15

DEVELOP CONFIDENCE IN YOUR SENSES.

Exercise: Don't listen to the morning's weather forecast until you step outside or stick your head out the window and let your body tell you the air temperature. In other words, take a guess; if you do this daily, by the end of two weeks you will be able to estimate the temperature like a native.

Exercise: When you're with friends, try to estimate their height and weight as compared with your own. You can ask them to verify your guess, if you're brave enough, but I'd add an inch or so to a man's height and shave a few pounds off a woman's weight, if I were you.

Exercise: Guess the time before you look at your watch.

Exercise: When you are riding in a car, take a guess (without looking at the dashboard instruments) at how far you've come since your last guess.

In other words, be aware at every moment that numbers are the symbolic representations of "how much?"—whether size, distance, time, or quantity.

Remember that Eratosthenes, who was born three hundred years before the Christian era, managed to calculate the circumference of the earth and the magnitude of and distance to the sun and the moon without a single one of the sophisticated measuring instruments that were to be invented more than fifteen hundred years later. And he was nearly correct in his calculations!

BRAIN BUILDER #16

START THINKING IN METRIC.

This doesn't mean that you think in inches and then convert the amount to centimeters. Forget inches. Simply *observe* in metric until you learn it naturally and painlessly. Thanks to the decline of the American dollar in world trade, more and more imports are coming into this country bearing metric measurements. For example, the label on your new wallpaper may tell you it's 71.12 centimeters wide. Don't peek at the rest of the label to see how wide that is in inches. Don't calculate it. Just take a good look at the wallpaper and absorb how wide 71.12 centimeters *looks*. In other words, "picture" things in metric without laborious conversion.

Exercise: Get yourself a "six-inch" ruler marked only in metric. If you can't find one, get one marked in metric and inches and mask the inch markings with tape. Use that ruler exclusively until you're entirely comfortable and familiar with it. It shouldn't take you long. Then graduate to a "twelve-inch" metric ruler and, finally, to a metric "yardstick."

Exercise: Do the same thing with a Celsius thermometer; cover the Fehrenheit markings with tape and use only the Celsius. Use the kilometer reading in your car in the same fashion. Remember, don't convert! Not on your fingers, not on paper! These are exercises designed to force you to think in numbers. (Of course, learning the metric system and the Celsius readings will certainly benefit you in case we ever do go metric.)

Let's visit with our old friends, the Kalahari bushman, the stockbroker, and the artist again, and see how they handle arithmetic, the beginning of mathematics.

Obviously, the stockbroker lives in a world dominated by numbers—3,000 shares at 220 and ⅞; up ¼, down ½. If you were to take away his pocket calculator, his desk-top printer/calculator and high-speed computer calc program, he could still function. There was, after all, a stock market before microchip miniaturization put a computer terminal on everybody's desktop. There are no mysterious calculations, no algebraic formulae, or equations for the stockbroker to worry about; pencil and paper could see him through with good old addition, subtraction, multiplication, and division. But the stockbroker has become accustomed to thinking in large numbers—when the market volume topped 185,000,000 traded shares, he was able to visualize those many millions, because a stockbroker can grasp the concept of a million.

Not so the bushman. His world is so contained that larger numbers are meaningless. He doesn't trade stock; he doesn't play Monopoly; he doesn't use money. Primitive people usually have no words in their vocabulary for large numbers—they need none. The Kalahari tribe has three words for numbers—"one," "two," "many." Other tribes, use "one," "two," "three," "five," or "many" to fulfill just about every contingency. "Five" is a good number for counting because there are five fingers (well, four and a thumb) on each hand and five toes on each foot. Let's say the bushman sees a herd of wildebeest and wants to tell others of his tribe how many there were. His eye is quick and practiced; whether he realizes it or not, he can do addition with lightning calculation. He sees, say, eighteen animals. That quantity represents to him the number of his fingers and toes (presuming he's held onto them all) minus two. If you took away six wildebeest, his eye would register that fact without stopping to count. The Kalahari bushman doesn't give it a second thought. Like the man who comes to estimate the carpeting, he knows what he's looking at. If the herd should be too large to count on his mental or actual fingers and toes, he could pile up pebbles, one for each animal, or scratch notches into a piece of wood. Both of these were real counting techniques among ancient peoples, and they served humanity well.

Our artist has "a soul above math," or so she thinks. Even so, she would never sell a painting for $200 if she thought it was worth $2,000 or let it go for $2,000 if she thought she could get $20,000 for it. She has grasped the concept that more is numerically identifiable and other concepts as well. Her artistically-trained eye recognizes in a split second the spatial relations between solids, where perspective lines meet, that parallel lines don't, and various other realities of the artist's craft that are based, whether or not she acknowledges it, upon proven mathematical hypotheses. The artist knows more geometry than she realizes.

The same thing applies to you. Even when you aren't adding or subtracting, you know the purchasing power of your paycheck and what will be left over by the end of the week. You know how much the federal government takes out, and how much goes to the state, and how much is removed as a contribution to your medical plan. You're familiar with the amount of your car payment, the mortgage on your house or the rent on your apartment, and what Susie's school tuition comes to annually. Whether or not you're comfortable with what those numbers represent in terms of meeting your monthly obligations, those numbers hold no fear for you because you don't picture them as numbers: you picture them as concepts with a size in dollars.

BRAIN BUILDER #17

ADOPT A NEW ATTITUDE TOWARD NUMBERS.

See them as what they represent. Approach numbers not as numbers themselves, but as recognizable concepts of "how much" or "how little."

Exercise: Cook something requiring a lot of ingredients, but don't try to measure them all exactly. Don't even use marked measuring devices. Instead, use an unmarked glass to handle the ingredients and measure by eye alone.

Exercise: Take a look around the house and find any problem that has mathematical elements, then solve it with drawings instead of with your calculator.

BRAIN BUILDER #18

As your motivation continues to increase, add mathematics books to your library.

Exercise: Add a good book like *Mathematics for the Million* by Lancelot Hogben (W. W. Norton Co.) to your intellectual first aid kit and use it, just as you are using your dictionary and the other reference books I've recommended. Read anything that interests you in the book for five minutes once a week. You can read for longer than that, but make it a minimum of five minutes a week.

Mathematics for the Million has the advantage over *Webster's New International Dictionary* of being fun to read. The more familiar you are with words, the more you will use them, and the same will hold true for math. Also, the more comfortable you become with mathematical concepts, the more easily you'll be able to transfer this newfound ability to nonmathematical areas.

Why do you think I asked you to read *Mathematics for the Million* for only five minutes each time? Here's the reason: You might find it so intolerable to even think about reading a book on mathematics for an hour or so each day or even once a week that you won't make the decision to even start the book. But deciding that you'll sit down with it for only five minutes and that you'll get right up again is quite tolerable. It's even tempting. That way, you can easily get started. And, if you have no wish to continue after the five minutes are up, quit without guilt. But do it again the following week.

This is a trick I used to get myself to the gym two or three days a week. I made up my mind that I would go on three chosen days for only five minutes. If I decided to leave after that, I could leave without guilt. I discovered that nearly every time, once I was there, I'd stay for awhile. But I always knew I could leave at any time after five minutes without guilt.

BRAIN BUILDER #19

TAKE TYPICAL PROBLEMS IN MATH AND
SOLVE THEM IN A NONTYPICAL WAY.

If the obvious method is to divide, see if you can come up with the answer "how much" by subtraction or some other way. The more methods you can use to arrive at the correct answer, the better. The more mathematical methods you employ, the better you will come to grasp mathematical reasoning. Try addition, subtraction, multiplication, long and short division, fractions, and decimals.

Exercise: Remember the little problem on the first page of this chapter? What is 12 divided by ½? How many different ways can you get the correct answer, 24?

BRAIN BUILDER #20

START SOLVING PROBLEMS YOUR WAY.

Take any simple mathematics problem in a textbook or quiz book—an elementary algebra problem will do fine—and work backward from the final sentence in the problem (the one just before the answer) to the first sentence. Often, problems in textbooks will be presented in such a way as to lead you slowly to the answer through more and more definitive information. However, you might not think quite that way. Try doing it from just the opposite perspective.

Exercise: If this doesn't work for you, try starting with the answer itself, plugging it into the last sentence, then working backward logically. This will offer you a perspective that you can't get by adding the answer to the straightforward method. In any case, the more ways you learn to solve the problem, the better you'll understand it.

HERE'S YOUR QUIZ FOR THE END OF WEEK THREE

1) If you divide a pie by ½, how many pieces do you have?
2) If you divide 12 pieces by ½, how many pieces do you have?
3) So how much is 12 divided by ½?
4) How does a mathematical mind help in nonmathematical areas?
5) What is the meaning of the word "discrete"?
6) What is the meaning of the word "discreet"?
7) Why should you "think" in metric, rather than "convert" to metric mentally?
8) Why should you "think" in Celsius rather than convert mentally?
9) What's the mathematics book I recommended?
10) Will using a hand-held computer ruin your ability to understand mathematics?

ANSWERS

1) 2. (And pieces this size will spell doom to your diet.)
2) 24.
3) 24.
4) It increases your ability to reason.
5) "Distinct."
6) "Circumspect."
7) It's easier. That's the way you learned the present system.
8) The same answer as #7, of course!
9) *Mathematics for the Million* by Lancelot Hogben
10) No. And using a wristwatch will not ruin your ability to understand time.

NOW HERE ARE THE ANSWERS TO THE 4-PROBLEM MATH QUIZ ON PAGES 59—67

PROBLEM I.

"Two stars and a moon = 10" says the problem; "a star and two moons = 8." Did you happen to recognize the simple algebraic problem there? 2x plus y = 10; 2y plus x = 8. What are the values of x and y? Less scary when you say it with flowers, isn't it? The solution to this easy arithmetical question is:

☆ =4; -○- =3; ✿ =5; ☽ =2.

PROBLEM II.

Did you work on that problem for more than 2 minutes without perceiving the answer? If you did, you need more grounding not only in logic and mathematics, but in learning how to analyze a problem by examining the data given. The answer is, of course, that there is no other dollar. You have been misled into remembering the $30 the room cost originally, when that has nothing further to do with the problem. Actually, the solution is this: The room costs $25, the three men have paid $27, overpaying by $2, and the $2 is in the collection basket.

If you perceived that fact right away, or within the first two minutes, you can solve mathematics problems more easily than you think.

PROBLEM III.

There's no hidden trick here—just logical arithmetic. Two for $10 and 3 for $10 do add up to 5 for $20 for awhile, but only until the 30 ties contributed by the "3 for $10" man are exhausted, and this will obviously be sooner than the 30 ties contributed by the "2 for $10" man. They will then have to delve into the supply contributed by the "2 for $10" man, actually selling some of them as 3 for $10, cheaper than they would be than if the "2 for $10" man had sold them on his own.

AND THE ANSWER TO PROBLEM IV:

$7,000.

CHAPTER
7

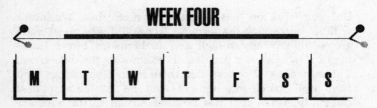

WEEK FOUR

| M | T | W | T | F | S | S |

Building a Logical Mind

TOOLS YOU WILL NEED FOR WEEK FOUR:
Paper and pencil and an open mind.

"Reasoning is as natural and familiar a process as breathing, but it is also a skill in which indefinite improvement is possible for anybody who is not a genius."

—Max Black, *Critical Thinking* (Prentice-Hall)

Why Do People Cling So Tightly to Wrong Ideas?

Why did I start the logic chapter with this riddle? Because I'm trying to make a strong point about *illogical* thinking, and how many people cling to it in the face of all the evidence that proves them wrong.

The logical person, being presented with an answer different from his own says, "Hmmmm. Let me follow the steps of the other solution and see if they work out. Well, what do you know? They *do!*"

The illogical person in the same situation typically says, "I'm so-and-so years old, and I've known the answer since 19-something-or-other, and I don't have to work out the solution because I already know it!"

Conundrums and riddles aside, this is one of the most common situations in everyday life—hanging on tightly to what one "knows" instead of opening one's mind and letting in the fresh air of simple logic.

Well, this chapter isn't going to turn into a textbook on logic, but it *will* introduce you to its defined approaches to the truth and give you some idea of how to use its precepts in everyday life and problem-solving.

Logic isn't something you leave behind in college. At least, I hope not. Because if you do, you'll have difficulty just getting through the day, not to mention accomplishing even the most modest of your goals. Living logically eliminates a lot of life's errors.

In his book *How We Think*, the philospher/educator John Dewey listed the following steps in establishing a logical approach to arriving at the heart of a problem and solving it.

The first step is to *become aware of the problem.* The second is to *define it and analyze it,* establishing its parameters. The third step it to *approach it rationally from different angles,* considering a number of options and various working hypotheses for its solution. And the last step is to *select a solution* and verify its effectiveness.

BRAIN BUILDER #21

THINK FOR YOURSELF.

Exercise: Don't just read problems when you come across them in print; solve them for yourselves. Here's a good one

77

to start with: A man is looking at a portrait on a wall and says:

"Brothers and sisters I have none, but this man's father is my father's son."

At whose portrait is he looking?

If you guessed "he's looking at a picture of himself," then join the club. It has thousands of members. And they're all wrong. The man is looking at a portrait of his son.

When I printed this puzzle in my "Ask Marilyn" column in *Parade*, I gave the correct answer without explaining it. And I had no idea what a storm of protest would arise. Letters began to pour in, hundreds of them, stating—some with passion—that absolutely, positively, the man was looking at a portrait of himself.

Here's an unedited sample:

WRONG!!! I am a senior at a university. Presently this term, I am taking a class titled 'THINKING.' Our Professor gave us the same riddle to figure out a couple of weeks ago. I was confused but did figure it out. Our Professor also confirmed the answer with us. The answer is: THE MAN IS LOOKING AT A PORTRAIT OF *HIMSELF!!!!* If you figure it out via a diagram it is easier. I hope to see a correction soon in your column."

B.K.

The answer to this poser is not the man's son but a picture of *himself*. This was a question in a test given to me in 1941 as an entrance exam for nursing. Before someone fails a test because of your answer, please correct it for them."

V.N., R.N.

Exercise: If your answer was wrong, solve that riddle again! Don't just read the answer—that's not the way to learn.

And when you've finished, here's the explanation:

I will call the man speaking "John" and the man in the portrait "Mr. X" and then phrase the sentence in a more normal conversational way without changing the meaning:

John says: "I'm an only child, and Mr. X's father is my father's son."

If John were to solve the puzzle himself, he could go on to say: "And just who *is* my father's son? As I have no brothers, it can only be *me!* Then Mr. X's father is *me*, and Mr. X is my son."

If we solve the problem ourselves, we must say that if John is an only child, and Mr. X's father is John's father's son, then Mr. X's father must be John. And if Mr. X's father is John, Mr. X is John's son.

BRAIN BUILDER #22

SEPARATE THE PROBLEM FROM THE SYMPTOM.

Exercise: Take a look at each of these common life situations and decide which illustrates a symptom and which illustrates a problem:

1) You're forty years old now, and you have to hold a book farther away in order to read it clearly.

2) You're forty years old now, and you get tired much more easily than you used to.

3) You have two children now, and your husband spends less time with you than he did before.

4) You have two children now, and you weigh twenty pounds more than you did before you first got pregnant.

The answers? #1 and #3 are problems; #2 and #4 are symptoms. Here's why:

1) A change in the ability to focus is a problematic, but normal part of the aging process.

79

2) Getting tired much more easily at the age of forty is not normal and should be considered a symptom instead.

3) If you now have two children, it's nearly impossible for your husband to spend as much time with you as he did before for the simple reason that you are probably offering him less time. And if he spends time with the children himself, that's even more time taken away from the two of you. The situation may be a problem, but it isn't a symptom of anything that isn't inherent in the circumstances.

4) Giving birth to children doesn't increase your weight, and if you weigh too much now, it can only be a symptom of another problem.

BRAIN BUILDER #23

DEFINE AND ANALYZE THE PROBLEM.

A large part of this is admitting the problem exists. But there's a key element to be remembered, an important part of using logic successfully in life. We must learn to approach problems rationally and not emotionally, or we won't be able to solve them. Hating a problem won't solve it.

Exercise: Using the above as examples, briefly define the problem. On #1 and #3, you've already had help; on #2 and #4, you're on your own.

1) You're forty years old now, and you have to hold a book farther away in order to read it clearly.

2) You're forty years old now, and you get tired much more easily than you used to.

3) You have two children now, and your husband spends less time with you than he did before.

4) You have two children now, and you weigh twenty pounds more than you did before you first got pregnant.

Now compare your answers with these:

1) You're simply growing older.

2) Unless you're ill, you're not exercising enough. To say here that you're just "not as young as you used to be" is to avoid recognizing the problem. If you were a hundred years old, it would be different. But you're not.

3) There is less time now to spend with each other. Saying "he doesn't appreciate me" is an emotional, not a logical response. There were no other circumstances detailed in the original problem to indicate that likelihood.

4) Unless you're ill, you're eating too much. Saying here that "motherhood changes a woman's figure," is, again, avoiding the recognition of the problem and the need to solve it. Motherhood may cause changes in a woman's figure, but it doesn't make her weigh more.

BRAIN BUILDER #24

APPROACH PROBLEMS RATIONALLY.

Exercise: Look at a problem from various angles and perspectives, then consider a number of solutions. Go through the four examples and find a few solutions for each, writing them down and making a special note of those that seem workable to you. Here they are one more time, but with the problems defined:

1) You're forty years old now, and you have to hold a book farther away in order to read it clearly. You're getting older.

2) You're forty years old now, and you get tired much more easily than you used to. *Unless you're ill, you're not exercising enough.*

3) You have two children now, and your husband spends less time with you than he did before. *There is less time now to spend with each other.*

4) You have two children now, and you weigh twenty pounds more than you did before you first got pregnant. *Unless you're ill, you're eating too much.*

Compare your solutions with these:

1) A. Read less.
   B. Learn to hold books farther away without complaint.
   C. Get reading glasses.

2) A. Choose more sedentary exercises.
   B. Stop vigorous activities when you get tired.
   C. Begin a program of exercise.

3) A. Look for companionship elsewhere.
   B. Spend more time with your children.
   C. Leave the children with a sitter more often.

4) A. Don't look in the mirror as often.
   B. Buy your clothing a size or two larger.
   C. Go on a diet.

BRAIN BUILDER #25

SELECT A SOLUTION AND VERIFY ITS EFFECTIVENESS.

In the exercise you've just completed, the solutions presented to you are ranked according to their effectiveness. The "A" group—reading less, choosing more sedentary activities, looking elsewhere for companionship, and making less use of the mirror—are all solutions of a kind, but they are short-range stopgap solutions and they will make the problem worse with time.

The "B" answers—learning to hold books farther away without complaint, stopping vigorous activities when you're tired, spending more time with your children, buying your clothing larger—are probably the solutions chosen by most people in real life, if not in theory, mainly because they are the default positions—the solutions involving the least change.

The "C" answers—getting reading glasses, beginning a program of exercise, leaving the children with a sitter more often, starting a diet program—are the most effective solutions that will effect a permanent change for the better.

Exercise: Take the solutions you've written and rank them in effectiveness according to the above groupings. Where do they fall?

Whether your solutions are solid is less important than in what group—A, B, or C—they tend to cluster. Do you tend to choose solutions that make things worse with time? Or that keep things the same? Or that make them better?

The logical solution makes things better.

Logical reasoning is something you will need to employ just about every day of your life. The more logical you are, the easier problems become, and the swifter and more painless their solutions. What you have learned of mathematical reasoning can easily be transferred to logical reasoning. They both work the same way, except that in logic, numbers are involved much less often, and when they are, they are not of such central importance.

BRAIN BUILDER #26

TAKE A CRITICAL LOOK AT STATISTICS.

The field of statistics is an area of transition from numbers to concepts. Consider, for example, the following results of a fictional survey of how average citizens feel about how the President is handling the budget:

Exercise: Can you find any other way to interpret the statistics below?

• 15% of the people polled greatly approved of his handling of it.

- 20% of the people polled approved of his handling of it.
- 30% of the people polled were indifferent to the subject.
- 20% of the people polled disapproved of his handling of it.
- 15% of the people polled greatly disapproved of his handling of it.

Looking at the above mathematically, we see that the range of opinion is evenly spread. That is, neither the positives nor the negatives predominate. This President could reasonably be said to be in a completely neutral position on his handling of the budget.

However, you could also extract the following statement from the above set of statistics:

"Sixty-five percent of the people polled do not like the way the President is handling the budget."

In that statement, you have added the 15% of the vehement disapprovers, the 20% of the disapprovers, and the 30% of the indifferent, who did not actually say they *liked* the President's handling of the budget.

This is not only an excellent example of faulty logic, it's something that's done all the time with polls of this kind in particular and with statistical analysis in general. It's been proven over and over that you *can* lie with statistics. It's all in how you add or subtract, multiply or divide.

The next time you take a look at a complete set of statistics, try seeing how many different ways you can interpret them. Often the best way to learn how to do something right is to see how and where you go wrong.

A tough mathematical mind will make you intellectually potent in virtually all areas of analysis. The analysis of any problem and the separation of fact from fallacy is the key to solving it. *And you don't have to know mathematics to have a mathematical mind!*

BRAIN BUILDER #27

TREAT LOGIC LIKE MATHEMATICS.

When you are facing a problem involving logic, treat it the same way you did the math problem in Brain Builder #19.

Try working it into chronological order. If that doesn't help, try rearranging it from the general to the specific. Think mathematically. That's the key to solving logic problems. In Brain Builder #14, we told you to think of mathematics as logic. Now we're telling you to think of logic as mathematics. The concepts are entirely interrelated. Clarity of reasoning can be derived from clarity of numbers. However, instead of "6 oranges," you think of "a box of oranges"; concepts take the place of quantities.

In everyday life, when you are confronted with a problem involving mathematics or containing logical or mathematical elements, move its factors around into a good sequential order—much like the way that problems are described in an elementary math text.

There are many ways to do this, so find the one that works best for you. You might try it first in chronological order. If the problem doesn't lend itself to time-framing, though, you might simply start with rearranging its components from the general to the more specific. This method often works, because problems typically flow that way.

Exercise: Use logic to solve this problem:

A frog fell into a well 32 feet deep. Each day he jumped 2 feet up the side wall and slid back down 1 foot each night. How many days did it take for the frog to jump out of the well?

This might seem at first glance like a math problem, because you see numbers in it. However, a knowledge of mathematics is not required to solve it; logic is. The presence of numbers in a problem doesn't make it mathematical any more than the presence of a frog makes it biological.

The answer? It will take the frog thirty days to jump out of the well.

To explain: Let's go back to the beginning and remove the distracting numbers. After all, the depth of the well isn't the point of the problem; the point is how the frog deals with it. Let's say instead that the well is only two feet deep. How many days will it take him to jump out? It will take him less than a day because he can land at the bottom, jump up to the ledge, and climb out. If the well is three feet deep, however, he'll jump up two feet and slide down one in the first twenty-four-hour period, then jump out as soon as the next day arrives, with only one day behind him. If the well is four feet deep, it'll take him two days, and so on.

THINK OF LOGIC AS EASY. IT IS.

Don't think consciously about dealing with logic the way you used to think about mathematics—as a difficult subject that must be learned. Instead, practice dealing with it more subjectively in the beginning, as a way to figure out things and situations that are relevant to your own daily life. Just as your feelings should change about mathematics, they should change about logic. Let's take a look at something called "modern deductive logic," which comes into play in many areas of your daily life. Deductive logic, sometimes called "symbolic logic," or (brace yourself) "mathematical logic," deals with the attempts to bring evidence in support of a conclusion. This kind of logic presents arguments in the form of statements (otherwise known as "premises") that must lead inevitably to the correct conclusion.

Here's an example of the simplest form of logical deduction:

Premise: All living, healthy, normal, human beings breathe through their noses.
Premise: Dorothy does not breathe through her nose.
Conclusion: Dorothy is a dead human being, a sick or injured human being, an abnormal human being, or not a human being at all, but something else (a goldfish, perhaps?)

This is a pretty primitive example because we still don't know who or what Dorothy is. Do we treat her injuries, bury her, or feed her ant eggs? Furthermore, the initial premise that all human beings breathe through their noses may or may not be true. But *if* it's true, and *if* the second premise is true, then the conclusion is true (although we need more data to determine the nature of Dorothy), and logicians say that the argument is valid.

Exercise: Imagine that you are standing in line, waiting to see a newly-opened and very popular film. It's ten o'clock at night, and it's very cold and windy. The film is not yet over inside, and you're waiting for the 11:15 showing. You are half-frozen and getting more impatient by the minute. The wait seems endless. How good a logical argument can you make for stepping out of that line and going for coffee or back to your nice, warm home?

Here's a good example of one logical approach to solving that problem:

Premise: In contrast to a live performance, all showings of a motion picture are identical to all other showings.
Premise: This particular motion picture will be shown many more times in the future when you can easily attend. Another showing of the film would do as well as this one.
Premise: Anybody who endures freezing and frustration for no good reason could use a 50,000-mile checkup on his brain.
Conclusion: Anybody who waits impatiently in the cold to see the very same thing he could see at a more comfortable time (when the weather is warmer or the film has played for several weeks and lost some of its crowds) could use a 50,000-mile checkup on his brain.

The point is, of course, that you can bring an objective logic to all sorts of questions, and it works equally well. If there is sufficient data in your premises, then your conclusion will be a valid one. Not only detectives in mysteries, but also computers work by deductive logic—"if such and such is true, then this must be the conclusion."

BRAIN BUILDER #29

TAKE NO PREMISE FOR GRANTED.

If you're having trouble with a logic problem, go back through it and see if you're taking anything for granted. Making assumptions is one of the places where you can get into trouble, not just in logic problems, but in life. If you can learn to stop doing that, it will stand you in good stead in both your professional and personal lives.

Exercise: Try this one: If all men named Ernest will date only women named Ernestine, and a man named Edwin has a party to which he invites three fellows named Edwin, four women named Edwina, one fellow whose name is Ernest, and two women named Ernestine, and if each woman named Ernestine meets a man who goes out to dinner with her afterward, what are the names of the people at dinner, assuming that one of them is Ernest?

Are you having any trouble with the solution? If so, go back through the problem and see if you're taking anything for granted.

Here's the answer: The names of the people at dinner are Ernest, Ernestine, Edwin, and Ernestine. I didn't say that women named Ernestine will date only men named Ernest, and I didn't say that men named Edwin will date only women named Edwina.

And saying that Ernest went to dinner on a double date with the two women named Ernestine indicates a tendency to be cute, a real problem, especially with bright people. They will sometimes become so preoccupied with strict interpretations that they will miss the overall thrust of the problem. This is what schoolteachers often call "reading too much into the question."

Logic Comes in Several Flavors

Sometimes the terms "deductive logic" and "inductive logic" are replaced by the Latin phrases "*a priori*" and "*a posteriori*," referring to two kinds of knowledge.

The Latin *a priori* literally translates as "from what comes before." It refers to the kind of knowledge we have already accumulated, facts we can take for granted from prior knowledge. Examples: cats mew, and dogs bark. Two and two don't make five, but four. *A priori* reasoning (otherwise known as "deductive" reasoning) is based on a set of assumptions we already have accepted as true.

A posteriori is translated as "from what comes after." In this kind of reasoning ("inductive") we must begin accumulating observable data from which we can then draw a general conclusion. For instance: every single time I have tried to walk through this doorway, I've banged my forehead good and hard. Obviously, I must be too tall to go through it without stooping.

TRY OTHER AVENUES OF LOGICAL APPROACH.

If you're having trouble with a logic problem at school, at work, or at home, add another avenue of approach. Try drawing a picture.

Exercise: Using simple drawings, answer the following question: Is the severity any greater *to the individual driver* in a head-on crash between two automobiles each traveling at, for example, 50 miles per hour, than one of them driving into a stone wall at the same speed?

If you're familiar with this problem, you may be able to repeat an answer you've already heard, but do you really know *why* it's true? Here are two pictures you could draw to find out.

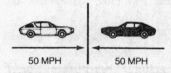

50 MPH   50 MPH

If you're in the blue automobile, you'll "share" a 100 mph crash with the green automobile to the tune of 50 mph each.

50 MPH

If you're in the blue automobile, and you hit a rigid wall, you'll get to "keep" all 50 mph for yourself.

In other words, to the individual driver, the severity will be roughly equal.

Putting it in writing might take a little longer, but it's much easier to work with concepts on paper in front of you than it is to work with concepts in your head. And you mustn't be embarrassed. Most of us can use this kind of help when we begin to exercise our minds, the same as we need help when we first learn how to exercise our bodies. Later on, you can do it in your head, if you like, although that will seldom be necessary. Getting the correct answer to a genuine life problem is more important than impressing people with your ability to do without paper. We don't expect lawyers to write a finished draft of a contract the first time they pick up their pens. Also, we expect them to refer to their law books when they do begin. Doctors don't carry their *Physician's Desk Reference* manual around in their heads, nor should they. If a doctor should attempt a difficult diagnosis based solely on his crowded memory without referring to any other sources, it ought not impress us; in fact, it ought to scare us away.

Neither should we expect this kind of "instant expertise" from ourselves. So far in this book I have stressed in various places the importance of not writing things down. Don't write down word definitions; take guesses, but don't write down the conversion of metric to inches, and so forth. These were exercises in building your brain power, exercises in the development of objective, independent thinking. But, when it comes to *solving problems*, the intelligent person calls upon every weapon at his or her command—insight, intuition, logical reasoning, experience—and pencil and paper.

BRAIN BUILDER #31

GET ENOUGH INFORMATION.

Granted, it's extremely difficult to know when you have all the available information, and even when you know you *don't* have it, you may not have any means of getting it and must still make a decision. If everybody waited until he or she had all available information before acting, we would make far fewer errors, but we'd never get anything done. This accounts for many of the errors in science. In small-particle physics, for example, the best conclusions would require information that can only come from instrumentation that is not yet developed.

But we can all benefit from trying to get as much information as we reasonably can before making a decision; or at least, make the amount of information appropriate to the gravity of the decision. Whenever it's advisable to postpone a decision until you have more facts on which to base it, do so without shame or hesitation.

Exercise: If all dogs have blue hair, and all cats have yellow hair, what do you call a creature with green hair?

Yes, combining blue paint and yellow paint does make green paint, but we aren't smearing the cat and the dog on the canvas. From the information given in the exercise, it would be wise for you not to call that creature anything at all, including a "dat" or a "cog." Try not to be intimidated into making a judgment on such insufficient evidence. Unfortunately, many of us make just such snap judgments on a daily basis, then cling to those conclusions because of our intense hatred of being wrong.

BRAIN BUILDER #32

FOLLOW THE PREMISES.

Keep in mind that the only requirement for the conclusion is that it follow the premises. The premises themselves may be true or false.

Why would you want a conclusion from false premises? Perhaps to gain a different perspective, such as "I'm a sergeant in the Marines, and I'm leading my men up a hill, but

if I were the leader of the enemy troops instead, and

if I were hiding a few men in that clump of trees,

then would I be forced to attack the Marines at the top?"

Following false premises to their logical conclusion is a good exercise in learning how to use logic.

Exercise: If diamonds don't scratch glass, and glass *does* scratch glass, which of the statements below are true if your engagement ring doesn't scratch glass?

A) It is a diamond.

B) It isn't a diamond.

C) It is glass.

D) It isn't glass.

E) It is neither diamond nor glass.

The answer is (D), and here's the explanation:

A) Just because your ring doesn't scratch glass doesn't mean that it's a diamond. It might be something *else* that doesn't scratch glass.

B) If your ring doesn't scratch glass, there is a possibility that it *is* a diamond.

C) But your ring can't be glass because it doesn't scratch glass, and glass *does* scratch glass.

D) According to (C), THIS MUST THEN BE TRUE.

E) According to (B), a diamond can't be ruled out, but we need more information to conclude that it's a diamond.

Supposing that the above exercise didn't drive you crazy, I'm giving you another one:

Exercise: If diamonds don't scratch glass, and glass *does* scratch glass, which of the statements below *could* be true if your new engagement ring doesn't scratch glass?

A) It is a diamond.

B) It isn't a diamond.

C) It is glass.

D) It isn't glass.

E) It is neither diamond nor glass.

The answer is (A), (B), (D), and (E), and here's why:

A) If your ring doesn't scratch glass, and neither does a diamond, it may be a diamond.

B) Your ring may be any number of things other than diamonds that don't scratch glass.

C) YOUR RING CANNOT BE GLASS BECAUSE GLASS SCRATCHES GLASS, AND YOUR RING DOESN'T.

D) According to (C), this must then be true.

E) According to (B) and (C), this may then be true.

BRAIN BUILDER #33

START USING LOGIC IN YOUR EVERYDAY LIFE.

It will come slowly at first, but the more you do it, the easier it will be. Ask yourself: *"If this is true, and if that is true, then is what follows a logical conclusion?"*

Exercise: Assuming you're not underweight, the next time you're at a restaurant, stop eating anything on your plate you don't like after the first bite or two, and put your knife and fork on the plate so the waiter knows you're finished. *If you've already spent money on this food, and if the taste isn't pleasing to you, is it a logical conclusion to use up precious calories on something you don't like?* You can either save the calories or spend them later on a favorite snack at home. If the waiter asks you if anything is wrong, tell him quietly and without emotion, "Yes, I don't like it." You might be surprised at how readily he may bring you something else, more to your liking, at no additional charge.

Exercise: The next time you're at a movie you don't really like, leave after giving it a fifteen-minute chance. You've spent your money; does it make sense logically to spend your time? And if the picture was actually offensive, stop on the way out and ask for your money back. You'll usually get it.

A Quiz to Determine How Logically You Think

1) What were the two kinds of "reasoning" methods mentioned?
2) What were the two kinds of "knowledge" mentioned?
3) What is one large part of defining and analyzing a problem in your everyday life?
4) Why should the logical solution make things better?
5) What is the difference between mathematical reasoning and logical reasoning?
6) Can you lie with statistics?
7) What are two other names for deductive logic?
8) A traveler is on her way to Delhi when she comes to a fork in the road. She is wondering which way to go when two men appear. One cannot tell the truth, and the other cannot tell a lie. The traveler doesn't know which is which. What *one* question can she ask which will show her the right road to Delhi?
9) A classic: A farmer had 17 horses he wanted to divide among 3 people. How did he do this if he wished to give one friend ½ of the horses, one friend ⅓ of the horses, and one friend ⅙ of the horses?
10) Which five U.S. Presidents are *not* buried on American soil?

The Answers

1) Deduction and induction.
2) A priori and a posteriori.
3) Admitting it exists.
4) If it didn't, it wouldn't be a solution, would it?
5) The former usually uses numbers; the latter usually doesn't.
6) Yes.
7) Symbolic logic and mathematical logic.
8) The traveler would pick either man, point to the other, and ask the first man, "Which road would *he* say is the right road to Delhi?" If the man who is asked is the truthteller, he'll indicate the wrong road because the truthteller knows the liar would lie about it. If the man she is asking is the liar, he'll indicate the wrong road, too,

because the liar would lie about what the truthteller would reply. Either way, no matter whom she asks, our traveler will know which is the *wrong* road and will therefore take the *other* road to Delhi.

9) The farmer borrowed one horse from a neighbor, giving him a total of 18 horses to work with. The first friend got ½, or 9 horses. The second friend got ⅓ or 6 horses. The third friend got ⅑, or 2 horses. The farmer then returned the remaining horse to his neighbor.

But whoa! Did you discover something wrong with the question as well as the answer? Good for you.

This question and its answer have been floating around for years, but the question is flawed because you can't give away *any* number by giving away ½, ⅓, and ⅑ of it. These fractions add up only to ¹⁷/₁₈ of the whole.

And the answer is just as bad. Bringing in extras for the calculation gives the friends more than the farmer originally wanted them to receive. Of his 17 horses, the first friend (the ½ share) should have gotten 8½ horses; the second friend (the ⅓ share) should have received 5⅔ horses. The third friend (the ⅑ share) should have gotten 1⁸/₉ horses. And the farmer himself would have been left with ¹⁷/₁₈ of a horse. The riddle, answered by borrowing a horse, gives the friends more than their share, and the farmer receives nothing. Even so, I think everybody would be happier that way—especially the horses.

10) The five who are still living—George Bush, Ronald Reagan, Jimmy Carter, Gerald Ford, and Richard Nixon.

CHAPTER

8

WEEK FIVE

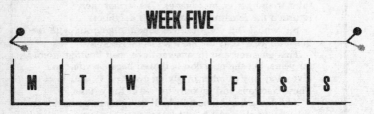

| M | T | W | T | F | S | S |

Building Insight and Intuition

TOOLS YOU WILL NEED FOR WEEK FIVE:

Your dictionary; a couple of paperback puzzle magazines that
include simple codes and simple number series;
a brand-new, unread detective novel of your choice.
Try not to be put off by the word "simple";
it's not meant in a derogatory sense.
A cipher or number series that is simple to those
who do them all the time will prove quite difficult for
the beginner.
So get the simplest such puzzles you can find.
If you've had a chance to buy your thesaurus,
that will come in handy, too.

"Eureka!"

—Archimedes

It's Saturday, and we're watching a "Road Runner" cartoon. The uncatchable bird is whizzing by in the canyon below, and Wiley Coyote is watching him from the cliff above, desperately hungry. If only there were a variety of birdseed that would slow the Road Runner down!

Suddenly, a light bulb goes on over the pathetic animal's scruffy head, and we in the audience know in advance that another big box from the Acme Company will be delivered to Wiley soon, containing the wherewithal for yet another foredoomed attempt to catch the Road Runner. This time he's ordered iron-filings birdseed and a giant magnet, but we laugh because we know it's hopeless, just one more in a series of vain attempts to attain the unattainable.

Although he doesn't know for a fact that Wiley Coyote is the one who has heaped it up in the middle of the road, with a sign on top reading "Free Seed," the Road Runner, when he stops to sniff it, will not eat Acme's doctored birdseed. Something tells him it's a bad idea. Without even seeing the magnet or tasting the seed, something has convinced the bird that the coyote's name is written all over this largesse.

That something is "intuition." The Road Runner doesn't have to employ logic or reasoning to come to the conclusion that a starving and desperate coyote is behind the offer of free birdseed; intuition tells him so. You might call this his "animal instinct," but if you did, you'd be somewhat off the mark. It's an easy mistake to make because certainly the two arise from the same physiology. But the distinction between instinct and intuition is like the difference between the autonomic nervous system and the central nervous system. Instinct operates almost independently of our desires or our reasoning powers, while intuition is more "voluntary." You, the Road Runner, and the Coyote are born with instincts, but you can develop your intuition. You can develop it and build it into a very important tool for delving into the deepest of life's problems.

And that light bulb that went on over Wiley's head? That was "insight," an insight that signalled the audience's intuition that for the hundredth time the mangy mammal hasn't a prayer of success and is once again flinging himself headlong into a no-win, no-eat situation.

Insight and Intuition: What's the Difference?

Although—just as with instinct and intuition—there is an overlap between insight and intuition, there is also a distinction between them. "Insight" is the clear perception of the framework of a situation—getting a handle on things. Although it, too, is innate—that is, it comes from within ourselves—it is fueled by factors outside of us: logic, reason, experience in similar or parallel situations. "Intuition" is entirely innate. It requires no reasoning, no logic, no rational thought of any kind. It is the immediate recognition from *within* of how, why, and the way things come to pass.

With insight we perceive obvious signals and put them together in a way that is not obvious. Here's a simple example: A monkey wants his soft teddy bear, but someone cleaning his room has put the toy up on a shelf he can't reach. However, the cleaning person has left a broom behind. Picking up the broom, the monkey uses it to knock the bear off the shelf and onto the floor of his cage. That connection the monkey has made between the problem and the solution is insight. It can be as simple as monkey-and-teddy or as complicated as Archimedes' discovering the principle of specific gravity while sitting in his bath.

What made Archimedes cry out "Eureka!" ("I've found it!") was an insight into the displacement by solids of a measurable amount of liquid—the insightful connection of the mathematician's body with the water in the tub. When many millions of people shelled out money for Rubik's Cube and turned that maddening little brainteaser this way and that in their frustrated hands, what they were looking for was insight, the connection that would make the colors fall neatly into place.

Insight: The Cognitive Leap

Insight—some may call it genius; others may call it "a cognitive leap." But I call it a combination of motivation, hard work, and perseverance. If necessity is the mother of invention, then surely insight must be the midwife.

It is possible, of course, to have a series of small insights and yet miss the most important one. The perfect illustration of this is Wiley Coyote again. In every cartoon, he gains one more insight (he thinks) into catching the Road Runner and sends away to Acme for one more piece of useless, cumbersome equipment. But the greatest insight of all continues to elude him, no matter how many bitter lessons frustration should have taught him. If poor Wiley depended more on his intuition and less on Acme, he would head straight for Pizza Hut; at least he'd get a meal.

The insight is that the Road Runner is simply too smart for him and consequently will never become his dinner. In addition, Wiley himself will inevitably be caught up in the mechanism of his own tangled plot and will be sent hurtling off cliffs, or blown to bits in some preposterous explosion, or dragged shrieking under the wheels of a speeding train. It is precisely that insight the audience possesses, and that's what makes us laugh.

BRAIN BUILDER #34

START SOLVING PROBLEMS YOUR WAY.

By "your way," I mean the one most comfortable to you and the way you usually handle things.

Exercise: Are you verbal? If you approach problems with words, then get out your dictionary and thesaurus and bolster your arguments with the most convincing and appropriate words you can find. Do you have a tendency to call upon a higher authority to bolster your claims? Look through your encyclopedia and find the pertinent articles to back up your argument with facts. Are you somebody who makes lists, writes things down? Then draw up the neatest and most concise list of arguments in your favor. Make sure you list them in descending order of importance.

BRAIN BUILDER #35

START SOLVING PROBLEMS IN AN *UNFAMILIAR* WAY.

Exercise: When faced with a problem, try to solve it in a way that is unfamiliar to you and uncharacteristic of you. In other words, not "your way." This is the identical exercise to the one above, but reversed. If you're comfortable writing things down, take the verbal approach instead. If you're somebody who always cites authority, make a written list without consulting anybody else, in books or otherwise.

The purpose of these exercises is not only to strengthen the insight mechanism you already have, but to give you glimpses of other useful methods that might work for you.

BRAIN BUILDER #36

TACKLE EVERY PROBLEM OR TEST OF INGENUITY
THAT COMES YOUR WAY.

Exercise: Be aware of *how* you go about solving it, which insights you form, and how successful they are. Even a difficult clue in a crossword puzzle will give you an insight into your insight. Do you hazard a guess at it? Do you look it up, relying upon a higher authority? Do you skip over it, hoping to fill in enough letters from other clues to lead you to the correct answer? All three? Other ways than those?

Exercise: On an intelligence test, there is a category for insight and ingenuity. Here is the sort of question that might appear in that category. Without using pencil and paper, can you answer it?

A mother sends her boy to the river to bring back exactly 3 pints of water. She gives him a 7-pint can and a 4-pint can. Show how the boy can measure out exactly 3 pints of water using nothing but those two cans.

Exercise: Okay, that one was fairly simple. But now that you have insight into the solution, can you solve the same kind of problem using an 8-pint can and a 5-pint can to get 11 pints? Then try a 4-pint can and a 9-pint can to get 3 pints. (Solutions are at the end of this chapter.)

Here's a real-life kind of situation requiring some insight.

Exercise: Your rich uncle Augustus is coming to dinner within the hour. You are his only heir, but you've just realized with horror that you haven't hung the little framed portrait of himself he gave you for Christmas. You hunt around for a hammer and nails, but you appear to be fresh out of both. The doorbell will ring in the next ten minutes, and Uncle Gus will expect to see his portrait prominently displayed.
What do you do?

Obviously, there is more than one solution here. You could, for example, clear off the mantelpiece or a small table and center the portrait on it as though that were the place of honor, not the wall. Or you could take down one of your other pictures and hang up Gus instead. You could use straight pins as a substitute for nails and the heel of your shoe as a substitute for the hammer. What other ideas can you come up with?

What's important here is not whether your Uncle Gus makes it to the wall or the table or any other place you suggest. What is major is how you tackled the problem and how quickly and successfully you solved it. How many viable solutions did you come up with? This is the role insight can play in your life, a simple example, but a telling one.

LOOK MORE CLOSELY AT "UNRELATED" THINGS.

Pay more careful attention to them than you usually do, and try to find something about them that is similar, ways in which they are alike. It's an exercise designed to encourage you to discover aspects of things you hadn't noticed before and is an important part of the process of strengthening and building insight. This is also a category of questions on intelligence tests, as, for example:

Exercise: How are a monkey and a banana alike? Here are three possible answers:

1. They are both living things.

2. They're both found in great numbers in Central and South America.

3. They are both considered food by the natives.

Can you think of any more?

When doing this exercise on your own, make as long a list of answers as you can, without being too facetious, as in "They can both be found lying on the bottom of cages at the zoo."

Then try these:

Exercise: How are a knife and spoon alike?
Exercise: How are a sauna and steam bath alike?
Exercise: How are black and white alike?

In all the above cases, state the obvious and then go beyond it, using your insight to build as long a list of similarities as you can.

LOOK MORE CLOSELY AT "RELATED" THINGS.

When you see closely-related things in your environment, pay more attention to them than you usually do and find pertinent ways in which they are not alike at all. This will also encourage you to notice significantly different properties of things that you may very well have been taking for granted, perhaps all your life. This is an even more important aspect of the process that produces insight. Here's a sample question:

How are "light" and "bright" different? Three answers:

1. "Light" has two well-known opposites; "bright" has only one.

2. "Light" is a more denotative word; "bright" is more connotative.

3. You can hold a "light" in your hand, but you can't hold a "bright."

What other answers can you think of?

Again, make as long a list as you can when you answer the following:

Exercise: How are a lobster and a crab different?
Exercise: How are kittens and cats different?
Exercise: How are onions and garlic different?

As you do the above two Brain Building exercises every day, make certain that your similarities and your differences are distinct from each other. Do not list more than one property of the same feature. For example, if you have said that a robin and a collie are alike because they are both animals, don't then write that they are alike because they're both living creatures; it's a given property of animals that they are living creatures.

OBSERVE WHAT LEADS TO INSIGHT.

Keep track of how you "scan" information in your daily life and how scanning leads to the formation of insight. The mental process involved in "scanning" for what comes next is a significant part of insight. In everyday life, you go through the "scanning" process when you're trying to remember a familiar name or recall a word from your memory. You "scan" —"I'm pretty sure it starts with *B* or *D*," you say to yourself—then "lock in" on the find—Barbara? Doris? Betty? Dierdre?—until the right name jumps out at you. This is single-step scanning, less complex than the multiple-step scanning commonly involved in insight; nevertheless, it's a useful kind of exercise because it occurs naturally and often. The trick is to be conscious of what you are doing when you're doing it and become aware of the frequency, rapidity, and method of your successes so that you can repeat those successes.

Exercise: The next time you're trying to scan for a name you know, but can't remember for the moment, try going through the alphabet mentally. In other words, take a quick mental look at each letter to see if it triggers the name from your memory. It should feel something like this: A? B? C? D? E? F? G? GEORGE! If that doesn't work by the time you've been through the alphabet, go back and do it again. If it's still not working after a couple of tries, go through the few letters that seem most promising, but in more detail. J? John? Jim? Jeremy? Jerome? Julian? K? Kevin? Keith? Kenneth? M? Matthew? Michael? MIKE!

WORK ON SOLVING NUMBER SERIES.

Number series—which are given on most intelligence tests and which you will find in a good paperback puzzle book such as those edited by Martin Gardner—are good basic practice because they focus your scan tightly, thereby making your search a little easier and helping you to define and hone the process.

The difference with number series and insight in general is that with numbers you must take extra trouble to "lock in" on a find, then proceed to check its accuracy. If your answer comes up incorrect, you "lock in" on another find, over and over until you find the one that really works, the one that satisfies the requirements of the series. By doing this repeatedly, you will learn to scan much more efficiently. Here's an example of a number series:

Exercise: 4   9   25   49   121   (?)

The correct answer is 169, that is, 13×13. And here is how to arrive at that solution:

The first successful step you take in your scanning process —your first insight into solving the problem—is noticing that the above numbers are all squares: 4 is 2×2; 9 is 3×3; 25 is 5×5; 49 is 7×7; 121 is 11×11. Therefore, the square root number series would read:

2   3   5   7   11   (?)

Scan *that* series, and your second insight will be that the above are all prime numbers, numbers which can be evenly divided *only* by themselves and by 1. Logically, then, the next number in that series would have to be the sixth prime number, 13. Going back to the original series, the answer would be 13 squared, or 169.

The following number series problems will offer you some practice. Now you know that your first step, your first insight is to determine what the given numbers have in common so that you can extrapolate that similarity to discover the unknown number.

The answers are at the end of this chapter, but try not to look at them, now or ever. If you don't solve the problems right away, scan again tomorrow and the next day, taking a different approach with each scan. The idea here is to strengthen insight and the formation of insight, not merely to learn how to solve number series.

Exercise:	2	9	28	65	126	(?)
Exercise:	5	25	61	113	181	(?)
Exercise:	7	22	52	102	180	(?)

The example we solved for you involved prime numbers and squares. The above include (not in any order) squares, odds, cubes, primes, and evens.

BRAIN BUILDER #41

LEARN TO PERCEIVE PATTERNS.

Practice breaking codes and ciphers and solving cryptic crosswords. This can be great fun for anybody who'd rather work with letters than with numbers, not to mention that breaking a code gives you a little tingle of power, a burst of pride in your intellect. Cryptograms, ciphers, and cryptic crosswords are readily available in newspapers and magazines. There are also paperback books of encoded cryptograms and cryptic crosswords (Penguin Books has a series of crossword puzzle books reprinted from the London Times, and each book in the series has a long preliminary chapter about how to solve the clues, which involves the development of insight into them). Like any kind of exercise, physical or mental, this starts out difficult, but becomes easier with practice.

Codes Are Mind-Stretching Puzzles with a Pattern

Codes are answers made into problems by intentionally obscuring the message. They have played an important part in history for thousands of years, especially military history. Only three of many examples that changed the course of history are the Zimmermann Telegram, a coded telegram sent by the German foreign secretary to the German ambassador to the U.S. in 1917 suggesting an alliance with Mexico in the event of America's entry into World War I on the side of Great Britain and France, the Japanese coded messages intercepted by the U.S. Navy that led us to believe there would be a sneak attack on our naval bases in December 1941, and the famous Enigma code used by the Germans in World War II and broken by the British.

The method used for encoding is always a pattern; it may appear to be a haphazard mess, but it is in fact a carefully selected but decipherable pattern. Decoding those patterns by slowly working your way to comprehension is an excellent way to exercise your powers of insight.

Here's a sample code, greatly simplified. As you start to solve it, be aware of how you are forming your insight.

Exercise: L LATSST IN IESR OH ECAR A EKIL SIEMO HT ASU INEGA

Did you get the answer? How? By perceiving the pattern immediately or by working it through a cluster at a time? What was the word or cluster that triggered the solution? (The answer is at the end of this chapter, as are the answers to the codes below.)

This next code is a simple substitution code, with numbers taking the place of letters. The same number stands for the same letter throughout. What gave you your first clue?

Exercise: 19–26–5–22   2–12–6   4–9–18–7–7–22–13
18–13   7–19–22   14–26–9–20–18–13–8   2–22–7?

In the next two codes, the same simple substitution, only this time letter for letter with the same coded letter standing for the same plaintext letter throughout each code. There are two different codes used. The important thing is for you to perceive the pattern in each one.

Exercise: VS ABG, JUL ABG?

Exercise: AVS ZPV DBM BKXBZT TSBQS
MPX DBM'S ZPV?

CONCENTRATE ON RECALLING YOUR SUCCESSES.

Exercise: Every day, make a positive effort to call to mind some tricky problem you have solved, an agreement struck that left both parties pleased, or some interaction with another person that turned out well. Try to remember both the problem and your solution in the greatest detail you can. What was the insight that led you to this success? How can you repeat it in other situations?

Exercise: Become aware of the *ways* in which you are insightful—can you read other people's psychologies? Are you skilled in interpreting the fine print in the contract or the hidden meaning between the lines? Are you familiar with an outside situation that may influence or have some bearing on the case? Whatever your insight abilities, make every effort to identify them so that you can call upon them again.

START THINKING ABOUT WHAT YOU *DON'T* WANT.

If, when tackling a problem in your life, you cannot decide what you want, make a list of what you *don't* want. Sometimes negatives may be as useful as positives in forming insight. Sculptors have been quoted as saying that when they are faced with a block of uncut stone, they can perceive the statue imprisoned inside, and they attack the problem by chipping away the excess stone to "release" the work of art. If you start by chipping away at the unwanted excess, you have a better chance of perceiving the "statue" trapped in the heart of the stone—i.e., the solution to your problem.

Exercise: Are you writing in the margins yet? Well, use the margin on this page to make a list of all the things you really don't want to do when, for example, your aunt comes for a visit. When you see the list in front of you, what you *do* want to do should become clearer.

Intuition: Putting Signals Together

Intuition: this occurs when we perceive signals that are not obvious to others and put them together. Sometimes the perception of signals is subconscious, seeming almost instinctual.

Here's a likely example. A housewife hangs her freshly washed laundry out in her yard and leaves for the market, returning to find the wash strewn all over the place. "I just *knew* something was going to go wrong today!" she says. And she did.

Subconsciously she'd noticed that her next-door neighbor had a new puppy, and her instincts warned her he might be mischievous, but her conscious mind didn't make the connection between the little potential troublemaker and the clean laundry. Yet her intuition continued to trouble her vaguely, sending her signals that said, "Something bad will happen today."

Intuition is the perception that makes you yank a child out of the street and onto the sidewalk just before a speeding car turns the corner. Intuition is what makes a champion speller, competing in a spelling bee, correctly spell a very difficult word he or she has never encountered before. Intuition is what made Julius Caesar's wife Calpurnia beg him not to go to the Senate on that fateful day in March 44 B.C. when he was assassinated. Intuition in the neolithic era was a crucial tool for survival, but it's a tool we civilized folk seem to have abandoned. To build your intelligence, you will have to reclaim it and sharpen its edges.

Is it possible to build your way to increased intuition? Yes. With practice, your intuition can be sharpened and your sensitivity enhanced. Building your intuition will give you a heightened awareness of your life and, combined with insight, teach you how to read life's "fine print," which you encounter every day.

The Three Main Components of Intuition

Remember the components of intuition—common sense, sensitivity, and luck. By far the most important is sensitivity, which you will need in greater proportion than the other two. In the situation of the new puppy and the wet wash, common sense tells us that puppies are playful and can be mischievous. Luck put the puppy next door in the first place. But without the housewife's sensitivity, the intuition would not have occurred.

Had she "built" her intuition, our young housewife might have trusted her feelings, brought her insight to bear on her world, taken note of the new puppy with her conscious as well as her subconscious mind, and come up with one of a number of solutions resulting in a basket of clean laundry.

So sensitivity is the thing to cultivate, and here are some exercises to help you build it.

BRAIN BUILDER #44

START TUNING IN TO TIME.

Exercise: Stop wearing a watch or looking at a clock for one week.

In the math chapter, I told you to become aware of "how much" time had passed by guessing at it before you looked at your watch or a clock. Now, I am telling you to dispense almost entirely with timepieces for a solid week. Make a timetable for yourself of your week's appointments and urgencies—a meeting you mustn't miss, a plane you have to catch. See how close you can come to keeping those appointments without a timing device, using only your own heightened awareness of time. Because I don't want you to actually miss them, however, do this: on the first day, you may check the actual time 6 times, but no more. (Guess at it first, though.) The second day, no more than 5 times. The third day, 4 times, and so on down to 0 times. Animals have "body clocks," and so do people, but we are losing the use of them because we are letting them atrophy, depending on manufactured time-tellers. Get back the use of your body clock.

Mental Tools Extend Your Mental Reach

Remember when I said that using a calculator would not decrease your mathematical ability? How can I say, then, that telling time by a clock or a watch decreases your sensitivity to the passage of time? Aren't the two things the same?

No. Mathematics is a function of the logical, reasoning brain, which often relies upon tools to extend its reach. Your body clock is part of your *intuitive* functioning, and you should strip away all outside mechanisms and allow your intuition to develop its full range. Mathematics is an absolute—it is either right or wrong, black or white. Your intuition is a flexible, sensitive instrument that requires a different kind of honing.

As your sense of time improves, you will feel a "keening" of sensitivity, a triumphant feeling that will make you want to continue its development in other areas. There are two levels of sensitivity; the first, the "external," or sensitivity to your surroundings, is far easier to achieve. Here's another external approach.

BRAIN BUILDER #45

START TUNING IN TO THE WEATHER.

Exercise: Stop listening to the weatherman. Just as with time, this exercise was introduced in the mathematics chapter in a simpler version dealing with temperature as part of the development of your instinctive understanding of "how much." Now to carry this external exercise further, to increase your sensitivity to your surroundings. Instead of listening to your local weather announcer, pay attention to the sky, the clouds, and the winds. After only a short time has passed, you'll discover that you have been taking note of pertinent environmental cues of which others are totally unaware. You can learn to do the same thing with many other aspects of your surroundings, ranging from the appreciation of art and music to understanding human behavior. The key is to "turn off" the so-called authoritative voice of the clock, of the weatherman, of the critic, and pay attention instead to the inner voice coming from your intuition.

Exercise: Note in the margin what the weather is like right now—not just whether it's raining, but what the clouds are like, which way the wind is blowing, and so on. Do this once a day while you read until you've finished this book. You'll be surprised at how much you've taught yourself about the weather in that time.

BRAIN BUILDER #46

READ THE BEST OF THE MYSTERY NOVELS.

Exercise: At the end of each chapter, write down whom you suspect of what and why. After you've finished the novel, go back and reread your thoughts to see where and why you went wrong and right.

Not only is this exercise fun, but it's good for you. I'm not talking about violent thrillers, or police procedural novels, but instead I'm directing you to those elegant, clue-filled, intelligent mysteries solved by drawing conclusions, not guns. If you try to keep one step ahead of the detective in an Agatha Christie or a Josephine Tey or a P.D. James mystery novel, it will sharpen your intuition. The Sherlock Holmes stories by Arthur Conan Doyle never go out of favor, and rightly so. Holmes's methods are Brain Builders brought to life.

BRAIN BUILDER #47

TUNE IN TO YOURSELF.

Exercise: Start writing down your guesses and hunches. For the next month, make a few brief notes every day about what you believe will come of relevant situations in which you find yourself or in which you're interested. Will the plumber show up in the morning as he promised? Will your new secretary or assistant be good on the telephone? Writing down each of your predictions has a dual effect. First, you become better at predicting because of daily practice. Second, you become more honest with yourself because you can see your failures as well as your successes. In fact, going over your bad guesses can become a fertile way to bring your intuition to full flower.

World events, the endings of mysteries and thrillers, stock market ups and downs—keep a running record of everything you thought was going to happen. How many times were you right? How far off were you when you were wrong? What do you think got between you and a correct hunch? Can you pinpoint what distracted you or influenced you? This is a corollary exercise to Brain Builder #42, in which you tried to recall in detail your successful insights, and it's equally important for intuition-building.

BRAIN BUILDER #48

BECOME YOUR OWN INSTRUMENT OF MEASURE.

Before you turn to any instrument of measure, try to picture in your mind's eye "how much," using only your senses. Whenever you take a measurement, such as distance or height, make your guess first, then find out the correct answer using the necessary instrument. Pay close attention to the differences between your guesses and the correct answers. Are you always off by too little? Too much? Sometimes one or the other? Think of the correct measurement as the target and your eye as the arrow. Keep refining your guesses until you come close to the bulls-eye. You'll be surprised at how soon and how often you'll be on target, maybe even dead center. Before long you will be enjoying the benefits of heightened awareness and a sharper mind.

Exercise: When you are riding in a car, take a guess (without looking at the dashboard instruments) at how far you've come since your last guess.

"Internal" sensitivity, as opposed to external sensitivity, is more difficult to achieve, but it will give you a real glow of brilliance once you have reached it. It's an intellectual sensitivity to your own thought processes. By working to attain this second, deeper level, we pay attention to our minds the way we paid attention to the sky and the clouds, the weather and "how much."

BRAIN BUILDER #49

STUDY SPELLING.

Remember our example, on page [109], of the champion speller who encounters a tricky word for the first time in a spelling bee and spells it correctly through intuition? Of course there are rules that govern spelling, but it's unlikely that anybody but a dedicated teacher actually knows them all, and besides, they are riddled with exceptions. Our champion speller has a developed "ear" for a word, and that "ear" is part of intuition. The best way I know to learn the rudiments of the "internal" process is to study spelling. You can study methods of learning to spell, memorize lists of words, take a course in the subject, or even do all three. The more ways you approach it, the better. Yet possibly the simplest and least costly way is to keep pencil and paper near you, and write down difficult words that you *hear*. Guess at the spelling, and then look up the word in the dictionary to see if your guess was correct. Spelling is the kind of intuition that you can actually verify, which is something you can't do with other kinds of intuition. But bear in mind that your goal must be better spelling, not increased vocabulary.

Exercise: Try to find conversations that will have words that are new to you. For example, take tours in art galleries and science museums. Listen in at courts of law. Talk to people who are specialists in one field or another, and who often use specialized and unfamiliar terms. If you hear a new word more than once, write it down and look it up when you get home.

After you do this for a while, you will find that you can *sense* correct spelling without even knowing why, just as you'll recognize that a word is spelled wrong before you examine *how* it's spelled wrong. Eventually, you'll have a better ability to *feel* what's needed in a situation and to begin to transfer this intuition to other areas of your life.

The Fine Print of Life

As you build both your insight and your intuition, the time comes when you must combine them to read what I call "the fine print of life." Every day, you are bombarded by glowing promises from advertisers, politicians, clergymen, and others. You are called upon again and again to make decisions based on what others tell you. In almost every case, however, *what they leave out* is as important as what they say. Allow your intuition and your insight to lead you to discover what the pitchman doesn't tell you.

BRAIN BUILDER #50

TAKE NOTHING AT FACE VALUE.

If your intuition tells you not to accept something completely, listen to it. Use your insight to read the fine print or between the lines.

Exercise: Take one evening to concentrate on television *commercials* rather than on television *programs*. Try to pinpoint what the commercial is really saying and whether it's a fair message or grossly misleading. Stay with it the entire evening, working on another project and *only* looking up when the commercial comes on. It may change your attitude toward advertising.

Put Your Insight and Intuition Together

Here's an example of a recent television commercial and how it involves your insight and your intuition. It goes without saying that we have changed the names of the products involved.

The supposition: A group of ten doctors is told that if they were stranded on a desert island, they could take with them a supply of only one "pain reliever." They are offered Amalgamated Aspirin, an acetaminophen called Extra-Strength Cure-It-All, and an ibuprofen product named No-Pain.

The claim: Nine out of the ten physicians choose Amalgamated Aspirin. The commercial is, of course, paid for by Amalgamated Aspirin.

Your intuition tells you that something is missing here. You know that the Food and Drug Administration cracks down hard on such advertising, so you don't doubt that the test claim of nine-out-of-ten doctors can be substantiated by Amalgamated by means of verifiable statistics. But you also suspect that the test has been loaded in some way to yield those results. Now your insight comes into play.

You know that aspirin is an extremely useful drug; in addition to its pain-relieving effect, it reduces inflammation and fever. Recent research has indicated that aspirin can reduce the risk of stroke or heart attack, and a number of doctors have even put their patients on a regimen of taking aspirin preventively. But insight also tells you that all aspirin—whether Amalgamated or another brand or simply a generic version—is alike. It's all salicylic acid. Oh, yes, they can buffer it and coat it and press it into caplets, but aspirin is aspirin; for years, consumer activists have been telling you to buy the cheapest aspirin because it makes no difference.

So a reading of the fine print of this commercial would go something like this:

There's an excellent chance that nine out of ten doctors *would* select aspirin to take with them to that mythical desert island, but would they necessarily select *Amalgamated Aspirin*? Might they not choose instead a different brand or even a generic, made to federal government specifications but costing a fraction of Amalgamated's price? Ah, but no other brand of aspirin, nor a generic, was offered in this test to our stranded physicians. If they wanted aspirin, it was Amalgamated or nothing. In other words, Amalgamated, knowing that doctors are partial to using aspirin in more cases than for simple pain-relieving, has stacked the deck by pitting itself in a test against pain-relievers with fewer medical applications. Had they matched themselves against another brand of aspirin or no-brand aspirin, the results might have been very different.

Political "Fine-Print" Is Everywhere

Another extremely common "fine-print" situation is the charges that our politicians are always bringing against one another, particularly in an election year. The Democrats (or the Republicans) will tell you that under the Republicans (or the Democrats), federal spending has exceeded the budget by the largest figure in recorded history. And they will quote a number in the billions high enough to give you the collywobbles—especially if you're against deficit spending. But there's something you know intuitively about a person who tells you something for a reason that might have something to do with personal gain. "Cui bono?" as Cicero asked. "Who stands to profit?" So let's bring our newly-built insight to bear and take a closer look. Numbers are as easily manipulated as words, by leaving out as much information as is volunteered. When you check the actual figures in their total context, you discover that, while the *amount in dollars* was indeed the greatest deficit figure in American history, the budget itself was also the largest budget ever presented to Congress. The *percentage* of deficit spending was actually the *lowest* ever. Politicians are confident that very few Americans will question impressive statistics, but anybody who takes the claims of any party's politicians on any important topic at face value deserves the government he gets. One of the most important aspects of building your mind, especially your insight, is to be able to use it to ask the right questions.

As you work on the Brain Builders in this chapter, you will begin to feel a kind of peripheral intellectual vision, a greater trust in your own abilities and capabilities, and a sense that you can grasp and make successful use of everything within your range—and even begin to extend it!

A QUIZ FOR WEEK FIVE

1) What quality does Wiley Coyote usually exhibit?
2) What quality does the Road Runner usually exhibit?
3) Is insight mystical?
4) Is intuition mystical?
5) What did Archimedes discover while sitting in his bathtub?
6) And was this discovery insight or intuition?
7) What does this book say is the most important component of insight?
8) What does this book say is the most important component of intuition?
9) What are the two levels of sensitivity mentioned?
10) What was that quote of Cicero's? (A hint: Law enforcement officers routinely use this one—although not usually in Latin!)

ANSWERS

1) Insight.
2) Intuition.
3) No.
4) No.
5) The principle of specific gravity.
6) Insight.
7) Motivation, hard work, and perseverance.
8) Sensitivity.
9) External and internal.
10) "Who stands to profit?"

ANSWERS TO THE PROBLEMS IN THIS CHAPTER

Page 101: To get 3 pints of water from a 7-pint can and a 4-pint can, fill the 7-pint can and from it fill the 4-pint can. What remains in the 7-pint can is exactly 3 pints.

To get 11 pints using an 8-pint can and a 5-pint can, fill the 8-pint can and from it fill the 5-pint can. Empty the 5-pint can, and you are left with 3 pints in the 8-pint can. Pour them into the 5-pint can and fill up the 8-pint can again.

To get 3 pints using a 4-pint can and a 9-pint can, fill the 4-pint can three times and empty it into the 9-pint can. The first two times will give you 8 pints. The third time, the 9-pint can will hold only one more pint, leaving 3 pints in the 4-pint can.

Page 105: The number series:

2	9	28	65	126	(?)

The correct answer is 271, obtained by taking each number in the sequence 1 2 3 4 5 6 to the third power and then adding 1.

5	25	61	113	181	(?)

The correct answer is 265, obtained by taking all the odd numbers in sequence from 1 through 11 (1, 3, 5, 7, 9, 11), squaring them, and then adding the squares of the following even numbers in sequence from 2 through 12 (2, 4, 6, 8, 10, 12).

7	22	52	102	178	(?)

This is much more complicated, but a lot of hard insight will reveal a regular pattern here. The correct answer is 286 and is derived thus:

2	3	5	7	9	11	(first 6 prime numbers)
		plus				
1	2	3	4	5	6	(first 6 squares)
		plus				
1	2	3	4	5	6	(first 6 cubes)
		plus				
1	3	5	7	9	11	(first 6 odd numbers)
		plus				
2	4	6	8	10	12	(first 6 even numbers)
		=				
7	22	52	102	178	286	

Page 107: The codes, ciphers, cryptograms

L LATSST IN IESR OH ECAR A EKIL SIEMO
HT ASU INEGA.

Answer: A GENIUS AT HOME IS LIKE A RACE HORSE IN
ITS STALL.
This code is deciphered by simply reversing the order of
letters in the entire sentence while keeping the original
word spacing. What was your first insight into the solution? Was it EKIL, which is the only word in the code that
has the same spacing as its reversal and which *looks* like
LIKE spelled backward?

19–26–5–22   2–12–6   4–9–18–7–7–22–13
18–13   7–19–22   14–26–9–20–18–13–8   2–22–7?

The answer is: HAVE YOU WRITTEN IN THE MARGINS
YET?
Here are some typical insights into solving this puzzle. You know that there are 26 letters in the alphabet, and
you notice that no number above exceeds 26, so you're
pretty sure that the letters they represent are in some kind
of alphabetical order. But starting where? Your first guess
is A = 1, B = 2, and so forth, but that doesn't seem to work
out. Your next guess would probably be: A = 26, B = 25,
C = 24, and so on down to Z = 1, and that's true. Another
clue: Guessing at the common word "the." 2–12–6 is a
three-letter word, but you can't get "the" out of it. But look:
7–19–22 is rich with meaning. If you assign "T = 7, H = 19,
E = 22," then in 4–9–18–7–7–22–13, you immediately get:
4–9–18–TTE–13, which would make 13 a good bet to be N,
D, or R; and the last word would immediately be 22–ET? So
22 narrows down to L, M, N, P, S, Y, G, or B, and possibly J
or V. The question mark is also a good clue for the first
word in the sentence, but you won't always be lucky enough
to be handed punctuation in a cryptogram.

VS ABG, JUL ABG?

Answer: IF NOT, WHY NOT?
Here the question mark is of great help, narrowing down
the choice of the first word in the code to 2-letter interroga-

tives like "do" and "if." This code is harder not because the cryptic alphabet begins at the second half of the plaintext alphabet (A = N, B = O, C = P, and so on) but because you have many fewer letters to work with. But a good insight into this code would be the *pattern* of the code itself. VS ABG, JUL ABG? almost cries out for IF NOT, WHY NOT? Identifying the pattern is, of course, the most important step in achieving insight.

AVS ZPV DBM BKXBZT TSBQS MPX DBM'S ZPV?

The answer: BUT YOU CAN ALWAYS START NOW, CAN'T YOU?

The first clue you might perceive here is the structure of DBM'S, which tells you right away that S is either S (as in man's) or T (as in can't, don't, won't). It's unlikely that S would be S in a code, so try T, which will also give you the N before the apostrophe (N = M) and tell you that B is either A or O. If B = A and N = M, the pattern becomes obvious: A = B, B = A; C = D, D = C; E = F, F = E, and so on, leading to the entire solution.

The bottom line here is to go for the pattern. Look for anything that suggests a pattern (such as DBM'S), and work from that.

CHAPTER

9

WEEK SIX

| M | T | W | T | F | S | S |

Building Orientation

TOOLS YOU WILL NEED FOR WEEK SIX:
A wall map of the area in which you live; your address book;
a pocket compass; an old appliance you don't mind throwing
away.

"... The *solid* earth! The *actual* world! The common *sense*!
Contact! Contact! Who are we? *Where* are we?"

—Henry David Thoreau, *The Maine Woods, Ktaadn*

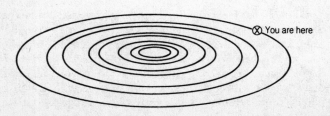

⊗ You are here

Hands up all of you who, when you were in grade school in those pre-Zip Code days, wrote your name and address into your notebook in a pattern like this?

> Johnny Jones
> 123 Main Street
> Minneapolis
> Minnesota
> U.S.A.
> North America
> The Western Hemisphere
> Planet Earth
> The Solar System
> The Milky Way
> The Galaxy
> The Universe

I did, and I'll bet quite a few more of you did. Children are curious about their exact place in the scheme of things. They seem to have an instinct for pinpointing themselves in relation to their surroundings that they seem to lose as they grow older. It's a real pity, because a sense of orientation in anything you do builds real intellectual fitness and confidence. It's like the orientation you possess in a familiar city. You may not know where everything is, but you know where you stand, you know where to look, and you are unlikely to become lost, or, if you do, to stay lost. The most important thing is that you have a grasp of the overall picture and can see yourself in it, your physical place, as opposed to feeling as though you were peering helplessly out at overwhelming confusion.

Don't Be a Passenger in Life

You know that feeling you have when you visit somewhere on a regular basis, but are always driven to it by somebody else? You never know exactly where you are. As a passenger, you're lost. What you need to do is to get into the driver's seat. You can learn better when you are in the driver's seat with a knowledgeable passenger than you can when you are the passenger with a knowledgeable driver.

That's another reason you should be writing in the margins of this book—to scoot over closer and closer to the driver's seat until the steering wheel is in your own hands.

Don't be a passenger in life. Don't merely follow somebody else's directions. The directions may be excellent, but they're not yours. At some point, you've got to do it yourself, go off on your own, and under your own steam. (Even if you take a few wrong turns now and then.)

For the purposes of the Brain Building program, there are three levels of orientation, listed in order of increasing difficulty: *physical orientation, mental orientation, and intellectual orientation.*

The Steps to Intellectual Orientation

Physical orientation entails seeing *where* you find yourself in your surroundings. This means you have to learn about your surroundings before you can place yourself within them.

Mental orientation is a bit more difficult. It requires attention to more than what your eyes see. It requires orientation to things such as days and dates. If you're not sure what day it is, you're wandering on the edge of the woods. If you don't know what month it is, you've taken the wrong path and all the trees are starting to look alike. And if you're still writing the wrong year on your checks every February, the robins will come and cover you with leaves.

Intellectual orientation is a combination of the first two, producing what we'll call *situational orientation*. With this kind of orientation, you're aware of both the seen and the unseen environments, which affords you the capacity to act with as much power thinking as is needed for the situation.

The Steps to Complete Orientation

Take these examples:

A dog is usually very well-oriented physically. Not possessing the capacity to orient himself mentally, his abundant energy is totally focused on his physical environment. He is keen to the slightest movement; he can find his way home much better than you can, but his mental orientation

124

is weak. If you were to hold up a new toy and show it to him, he would be all thump-tail and eager-paws. But put that toy behind your back where he cannot see it, and he won't know where to begin to look. Once it's left his physical environment, it becomes out of sight, out of mind.

We all know somebody who is very well-oriented mentally. He has memorized the dates of every significant event in the recent past. He doesn't bother to carry an address book because he knows everybody's address and telephone number by heart. He jumps around eagerly in his seat until the instructor calls upon him to work a math problem on the blackboard in front of two hundred fellow students. Yet, intellectual as he appears to be, there's something very odd about him—his ill-fitting clothes are thrown on haphazardly, with no correlation of style and pattern; he gets tired just *watching* other guys working out at the gym; he very seldom has a date. Out of mind, out of sight.

Don't be too impressed with Mr. Nerd's feats of memory. When so few interesting things happen in your own life, it's a lot easier to remember the dates of them all, and even add the dates of historical events. Ask yourself how hard it is to remember telephone numbers and addresses when you have only a half-dozen or so people in your life who'll have anything to do with you. As for the brilliant solution to those blackboard math problems, well, one can get a lot of math practice in on a succession of long, lonely Saturday nights. Mental orientation by itself, like physical orientation alone, is only the beginning of the battle. The trick is to combine them to your own advantage and use them in building your brain power.

But the person who is capable at both physical and mental orientations has genuine intellectual orientation. This is the person who literally knows where he or she stands in the universe, who can take what life dishes out, and who can handle most situations and encounters with calm assurance. This is the man or woman who can participate in significant financial discussions for the company during the day on Friday and entertain an entirely different kind of company on Friday night. This is the man or woman who can negotiate both a million-dollar deal and a new slope at Aspen.

What direction are you facing now, as you read this? If you are in familiar terrain, but don't know or cannot figure it out almost instantly, we have our work cut out for us. Let's begin building your physical orientation:

ORIENT YOURSELF IN YOUR CITY.

Exercise: Get a good wall map of your city and put it up in a handy place. If it's an axonometric projection of your city, showing the buildings and features at an angle to indicate three dimensions, so much the better. Keep the map next to your desk or by your telephone or some other place where you can study it daily. Find your home on the map, and take your bearings. Are you facing northeast or southwest? Where is your home in relation to City Hall? To your favorite movie house or restaurant? Which of your windows face due east? To what direction does the front door open?

Exercise: Go through your address book and determine where everyone stands in relation to you. Does your dentist practice to the northeast or the northwest? Does your yoga instructor live to the southwest or southeast? Does your zither class meet to the east? The west?

ORIENT YOURSELF IN YOUR WORLD.

Exercise: Buy yourself a very small pocket compass and carry it with you for a while. Orient yourself, like a sailor, to "true north." Always be aware of where north is and what direction you're facing, especially when you are in or going to some place new to you. Check your compass until you have learned its directions so well that it has become second nature to you and you can do without it. Remember that the point of the exercise is not where north is, but where *you* are. The desired result is to orient you to your surroundings, whether familiar or new.

126

Exercise: From now on, at least once a week give a set of directions using the points of the compass, not the gas station on the corner. Don't say, "Turn left at the first light." Instead, say, "Turn *south* at the first light." Passing along directions like these will force you to orient yourself. If nobody asks you for directions, tell them where to go anyway! You can even tell the kids something like, "Go out the front door, walk north, pick up the hose, walk south, and water the zinnias."

BRAIN BUILDER #53

GET HIGH.

All right, everybody had a good laugh, but the point is that three-dimensional orientation is better for your understanding than two-dimensional. Whenever you can, go up to the top floors of tall buildings and look out the windows, checking for landmarks you recognize and the direction you're facing. Get up in the air whenever possible. When you're on vacation, pass up the all-day ground tour and take the half-day air tour instead. Or ride up and down in glass elevators, especially in buildings that have them facing in all directions.

Exercise: At least once a month, resolve to get off the ground floor and up as high as is reasonably convenient. Is there a restaurant on the top floor of a tall building nearby? Try it for lunch, and be certain to spend as much time as possible looking out the window. Is there some kind of very tall tourist attraction in your city that you've always meant to get around to seeing, but haven't because you live right there? Visit it. If there isn't one, at least take the elevator to the top floor of the next tall building you find yourself in, and look out the windows for a while. Look at it this way. Suppose, while you are on the ground, you walked only from side to side, never back and forth. You would be losing what amounts to a dimension, walking in Flatland—a two-dimensional universe—instead of the real world. In the real world, we aren't restricted in our movements like chess pieces on a board; we can make *all* the moves. By going aloft to look down at our neighborhood, our city, and our world, we add *depth* to our orientation and give it contour.

GET OUT.

Exercise: Take part in a sport or physical activity that actively involves the landscape. An exercise bike may be good for physical health, but a bicycle ride through the park, the countryside, or around the city is better for the intellect and the judgment. Similarly, jogging outdoors is better for building your brain power than aerobics in a gym, and swimming in the ocean is more mentally stimulating than swimming in a pool. Outdoor activities require considerably more orientation of your body to its surroundings than do indoor sports.

Exercise: At least twice a month, exercise outdoors.

GET INTO UNFAMILIAR SITUATIONS.

A good friend of mine, who has a country home, is constantly driving down unfamiliar back roads, certain that they'll eventually lead to familiar county routes and highways. As a result, he not only knows every shortcut and every striking piece of local scenery, he is always totally oriented when he's behind the wheel, even when he's a passenger. He can tell you at any moment whether the road is winding northeast, south, or due west. Let's say you're on a lake in a little motor boat, fishing there for the first time. At the end of the day, while there is still plenty of daylight, put away your rod and reel, turn on the motor, and spend half an hour exploring the place.

Exercise: Get lost a few times a year. One good way to do it safely is to go with a friend who knows the territory. That is, take a walk in the woods near a friend's house, but ask your companion not to guide you in any way. See if you can find your way back without assistance, using only your senses and your observations of landmarks and surroundings. That way, you will become more sensitive to your environment and still be on time for dinner.

Exercise: The next time you find yourself lost, stop and relax before asking for help. (Unless, of course, you're in some sort of danger.)

Being lost can be frightening, like awakening in a strange place at night and not knowing for a moment where you are. It's disorienting. But the more comfortable you are in unfamiliar surroundings, the more confident you will feel. The next time you find that you've lost your way, take a deep breath and experience your feelings. Get used to them. You might even learn to enjoy "discovering" unfamiliar surroundings!

BRAIN BUILDER #56

Stop relying on maps.

Exercise: Combine an exercise with a day out. Decide where you want to go, look only once at the map, then go!

Use your eyes, your memory, and your sense of orientation instead. When somebody gives you directions to a new place, write them down, read them through, and carry them with you, but try not to use them unless you're lost and/or running out of time. The same goes for maps. Check the map before setting out, figure out how you're going to get where you're headed, then put the map away and simply concentrate on getting there.

BRAIN BUILDER #57

DON'T BE AFRAID TO GET LOST.

The fear of getting lost is very restricting, both physically and mentally. Unless you're in the rare situation where getting lost will actually be a threat to your health or safety, move around freely and explore your surroundings. If you don't trespass and you're not in a dangerous area, what could possibly happen to you? You might even consider deliberately getting lost—in controlled situations—to confront the fear and get used to dealing with it.

Exercise: Go to the largest complex of public buildings you can find and try your best to get lost inside. Then use your wits to find the way back out without asking anyone for help.

The building of physical orientation is of a piece with a number of other Brain Builders on which you've been working—becoming attuned to the passage of time, knowing the weather without a professional forecaster, and so on. Can you see the pattern emerging here, the result toward which we're all working? It's a sharpening of your senses and sense of self, a rejection of ready-made and manufactured "authority," such as clocks and maps and thermometers, a development of and reliance upon your own independent thinking and a trust in your own instincts. As you're developing a total feel for your physical environment and your particular situation in that environment, let's turn to mental orientation:

BRAIN BUILDER #58

ORIENT YOURSELF IN TIME.

Banks and other companies often hand out free little plastic wallet-sized calendars with a full year printed on one side. A year is the time period very commonly used in our society, and you should become oriented within it. Knowing merely what day of the week it is will be too narrow. You should also know what week of the month it is, which means you should either always know the date—which pegs the week exactly—or at least know if you're in the first, second, third, or fourth quarter of the month. Get yourself a month-at-a-glance calendar and note significant events and activities in it.

Exercise: Get a calendar that shows a full year at a glance, and note big events on it—important deadlines, when your cast is due to come off, when your mother-in-law's coming to visit, vacations, even the opening of baseball season, if you're a fan. In other words, try to stop orienting yourself within the next week or two and start orienting yourself within a much larger scope.

BRAIN BUILDER #59

PLAY GAMES.

Exercise: Go out to a good game store and buy just one game that you think you'd enjoy. I'm not talking about *Trivial Pursuit* or gin rummy or any other game requiring you to memorize facts or keep track of which cards have already been discarded; nor am I talking about games of chance, where results follow the fall of the dice. What we need here are games that are tough on the intellect, that require you to think hard before you make a move. I recommend chess, but if you don't know chess, checkers will do. Even Scrabble is a good choice for this Brain Builder. Any game that requires you to strategize, to project yourself into future time, to think ahead several moves, and to try to outguess and out-think your opponent is suitable for this exercise.

What you should concentrate on here is the process, not the outcome, although a well-thought-out process will often lead you to victory. How many moves ahead could you foresee? Were you aware of your opponent's strategy throughout the game or only sporadically? As each new game begins, resolve to s-t-r-e-t-c-h your mind further into the future than you did in the game before.

Take any kind of intelligence test you can find, even the basic ones. *Ignore the answers if they're printed elsewhere, and ignore the instructions—particularly the time limits.*

Treat each question as a game or a separate mental exercise, and stay with it until you solve it. Don't use the answers to grade yourself against others or give yourself a numerical score. What you are after here is not only your personal best, but r-e-a-c-h-i-n-g further to gain it. Your reach should always exceed your grasp, but if you look back over your shoulder, you'll see how far down the road to power thinking you've already come.

Intellectual Orientation—a Step into the Third Dimension

You have a new sense of yourself in both time and space; at any given moment you know better than before where you are and what comes next. That's more than many people know.

Now let's put your physical and mental orientations together to make intellectual orientation. Here we go further into three dimensions:

TAKE THINGS APART.

Exercise: Make it a habit not to throw things away until you first take them apart to see how they work. Instead, keep an old clock or something of that kind in your closet until you have a little spare time or—and this can be very satisfying—until you feel irked or angry about something. Then take the thing apart, and remember to have fun doing it. After all, you don't have to worry about breaking it.

BUILD SOMETHING.

Build something real, not a model or a miniature, but something with a function and a useful purpose, and put it to that use, even if it's nothing more complicated than a bird-house or a platform bed for your dog. Before you pick up a tool, sit down with paper and pencil and *plan* it. If you can, draw a blueprint, no matter how simple, with measurements clearly marked on the paper. Think about every element that goes into the job: what are the right kind of nails, and do you want to use nails or screws? Does it have to be watertight? Must it fit into a confined space? Will enough air get in, if air is what you want? Does it need to be polyurethaned? Look into the future and actually see it in use. Be aware of every step in the project's development as it comes to three-dimensional life under your hands.

The next time you employ workmen, especially in the building or renovation of your house or apartment, be involved in every step from planning to hammering in the final nails. The idea is to gain an understanding of the surroundings you've been taking for granted all these years.

Exercise: Write down—in the margin, of course!—a few things you might reasonably be able to construct in a minimum amount of time.

BRAIN BUILDER #62

BECOME MORE ACTIVE.

Get yourself involved in a team sport or one that you can play with another person. People are very, very much a part of the physical landscape, and interacting with them is essential to good situational orientation. Basketball and tennis, which require close attention to both the whereabouts of the ball and the whereabouts of the other player(s), are good for this Brain Builder.

Exercise: Go check out your local YMCA in person. Something may interest you once you're there. "Y" activities are a good, low-cost introduction to the active life.

An Orienting Quiz for the End of Week Six

1) What was illustrated in the beginning of this chapter?
2) And what's beyond the edge of the Milky Way?
3) What are the two steps to intellectual orientation?
4) What was the other phrase used for "intellectual orientation"?
5) What sort of map shows the features at an angle to indicate three dimensions?
6) Where on earth can you never move east or west?
7) Which direction are you facing right now?
8) Which direction does your bed face?
9) What's the best game for sharpening your intellect?
10) Who said "Contact! Contact!"?

Answers

1) The Milky Way.
2) Your scribbled notes should be there!
3) Physical orientation and then mental orientation.
4) Situational orientation.
5) An axonometric projection.
6) The North Pole and the South Pole!
7) I'm stumped. You tell me.
8) "Up" is an acceptable answer only if you're under twelve years old.
9) Chess.
10) Henry David Thoreau.

CHAPTER

10

WEEK SEVEN

| M | T | W | T | F | S | S |

Building Attention Span and the Senses

TOOLS YOU WILL NEED FOR WEEK SEVEN:
A guide to television programming; an alarm clock; some good
food; a few fragrant flowers.

"Attention is, in fact, a highly directed process. Shift the
focus of attention, the area of interest, and totally new sensory
data flow in. This shift depends on such things as alertness,
degree of concentration, and areas of interest."

—Richard Restak, M.D., *The Brain*

Before you can expand your intellectual horizons in the
areas of information-processing, comprehension, and perspective, it's imperative that you increase your attention
span and expand the perceptions of your senses. Think of
the brain as a switching center, like that of a giant railroad,
sending different trains down different tracks all at the
same time. You always want to be awake at the switch.

When one thinks "short attention span," one almost always identifies it with very young children, and that's as it ought to be. Toddlers are so curious about everything that they'll drop an activity in the middle to pick up something else that catches their eye. So do chimpanzees. But we adult humans should have enough *zitsfleisch* (a Yiddish word meaning the seat of the pants applied to the seat of the chair) to stick to a job until it's done, and with anyone of powerful intelligence, this is indeed the case. When building your own intelligence, building your attention span first is a critical factor.

Intelligence tests require you to correctly repeat a sentence you've just heard, the gist of a longer passage, and a series of numbers. Sentence memory, passage memory, and digit memory are based on the span of your attention and are tests of that span and how well you are able to focus it.

Let's Test Your Own Attention Span

Here are typical examples of sentence memory, passage memory, and digit memory from a standard intelligence test. You can take this little test by asking another person to read the sentence, passage, and number series out loud to you, neither too slowly nor too quickly, but clearly and in a natural rhythm. Concentrate on what you're hearing; it will probably be helpful if you shut your eyes to block out all visual distractions.

As your friend reads, try to picture the words as you hear them, written out on a blackboard. With the longer passage, concentrate on memorizing the key words. The others will fall into place by themselves.

The scoring on a test like this tends to be absolute—you receive credit on the sentence memory and the digit sequence only if you repeat every word of the sentence exactly, down to the last syllable, or the digits in their correct order, down to the last numeral. Muff a word or a number, and you receive no score. In a passage memory exercise, the scoring is again black and white, except you're not expected to remember every exact word. You are, however, given credit only if you can recall every salient point in the passage. You either get these right, or you get them wrong. But, on an intelligence test, as the sentences, passages, and number series become increasingly more complex and difficult, the test-taker will usually begin to stumble more often. At that point, the test is stopped, and the testee is given credit for the levels at which there were no errors. It works something like an eye chart, except that you don't come away with new glasses.

Ready? Then cover the rest of the page with your hand before you are tempted to look at it, hand the page to a friend, close your eyes, and concentrate on listening to the sentences, the passages, and the number series.

SENTENCE MEMORY.

Repeat the following sentences word for word:
Exercise: The superior man does not set his mind either for anything, or against anything; what is right he will follow. (Confucius)
Exercise: I have gained this by philosophy: that I do without being commanded what others do only from fear of the law. (Aristotle)
Exercise: None can love freedom heartily, but good men; the rest love not freedom, but license. (Milton)
Exercise: Every man takes the limit of his own field of vision for the limits of the world. (Schopenhauer)
Exercise: A man is not idle because he is absorbed in thought. There is visible labor and there is invisible labor. (Victor Hugo)
Exercise: Few things are harder to put up with than the annoyance of a good example. (Mark Twain)

PASSAGE MEMORY.

Repeat as much of the passage as you can remember. Keep the salient points in the same order as you hear them.
Exercise: People are always blaming their circumstances for what they are. I don't believe in circumstances. The people who get on in this world are the people who get up and look for the circumstances they want, and, if they can't find them, make them. (George Bernard Shaw)

Exercise: All this will not be finished in the first one hundred days. Nor will it be finished in the first one thousand days, nor in the life of this Administration, nor even perhaps in our lifetime on this planet. But let us begin. (John Fitzgerald Kennedy)

Exercise: A philosopher of imposing stature doesn't think in a vacuum. Even his most abstract ideas are, to some extent, conditioned by what is or is not known in the time when he lives. (Alfred North Whitehead)

Exercise: Not only does one not retain all at once the truly rare works, but even within such works it is the least precious parts that one perceives first. Less deceptive than life, these great masterpieces do not give us their best at the beginning. (Marcel Proust)

Exercise: We are inclined to confuse freedom and democracy, which we regard as moral principles, with the way in which these are practiced in America—with capitalism, federalism and the two-party system, which are not moral principles, but simply the accepted practices of the American people. (James William Fulbright)

Exercise: We are most likely to get angry and excited in our opposition to some idea when we ourselves are not quite certain of our own position, and are inwardly tempted to take the other side. (Thomas Mann)

DIGIT MEMORY.

Repeat the following numbers in the same sequences that you hear them. These sequences will become more difficult; continue until you begin to make mistakes.

Exercise: 0 3 8 5 0 4 7
Exercise: 1 6 4 9 5 6 8 3
Exercise: 6 2 3 8 4 9 3 2 4
Exercise: 3 9 6 4 9 1 7 5 8 2

Now try to repeat these series *backward*, digit for digit.

Exercise: 1 3 4 9
Exercise: 9 6 8 3 5
Exercise: 1 1 8 2 0 7
Exercise: 7 5 5 3 9 0 6

Number Series As an Aid to
Your Short-Term Attention Span

Did you have any trouble remembering the seven-digit series? If you did, make up about a dozen of them each day for the next week, practicing them until you're comfortable seeing or hearing a seven-digit series once, then repeating it once or twice. When you can do that with ease, you should be able to hear a telephone number once and have no problem holding it in your short-term memory until you actually dial it.

Although the word "attention" is singular, attention itself is not—there are several kinds of attention, each useful in a different way, and all necessary. There's the long-range kind of tenacity required to plow through and digest a boring, but necessary, corporate report and the creative kind of perseverance required to stay with an original project of your own. Too many half-knitted sweaters or unfinished letters are languishing in desks or closets because of insufficient perseverance.

Still other kinds of work require shorter, but more intense bursts of attention to make an extraordinary exertion of mental muscles or break through to new areas of thinking, supplying you with that final push that can make the difference between your reach and your grasp.

BRAIN BUILDER #63

TRY NOT TO WATCH TELEVISION.

Exercise: For just one day each week, don't turn the television set on at all, and that includes news programs. You can pick the evening, and you can even consult the program guide first, but don't turn the set on, not even for five minutes.

Television Versus Your Attention Span

Unfortunately, the rapid, staccato pace of modern life is the sworn enemy of a lengthened attention span and, in this war between them, the enemy's four-star general turns out to be America's second favorite indoor sport, television-watching.

We've grown up, most of us, trained to the artificially fast tempo of TV. Even the best of the children's programming, the most serious of the television documentaries, and the most professional news programs cover far too much in far too short a time.

Enormously complex social issues, such as the treatment of AIDS patients or the right of a terminally-ill patient to choose to die, are typically covered in a four-minute segment of the television news. Highly-regarded and much-watched shows like *60 Minutes* and *20/20* offer up stories behind the news, contained in 20-minute pieces of time, minus a few minutes for commercial breaks. These stories often pose almost unanswerable questions, ones which frequently challenge ethics or morality and which could stump a Solomon or a panel of Supreme Court judges. But television makes no such demands on the viewer's attention span; it's eighteen minutes for a major issue, then cut to a commercial.

One of the worst cases of "instant information" I've seen on television was a program that managed to condense not just one world war, but *two* to 60 minutes (48 minutes plus commercial breaks) of fast-paced entertainment. At this rate, all of recorded history could be shown to us in less time than it takes to do a weekend telethon!

In a recent newspaper interview, psychotherapist and family stress counselor Dr. Ross McCabe was quoted as asserting that he had removed the family's television set from his home before his children were born.

"About 90 percent of the programs are the most atrocious waste of time," said Dr. McCabe. "People get addicted to it. Information in that format doesn't do anyone any good."

Although he granted that television does expose children to the realities and the absurdities of life, Dr. McCabe added, "But it all ends happily in 30 minutes. It's ludicrous."

I agree with that. Yet I'm aware that the television habit is ingrained in most Americans, and you're not about to give your set away as McCabe did. But if you are serious about wanting to think better, and especially if you want to lengthen and strengthen your attention span, at least do the following:

Do these at home:

BRAIN BUILDER #64

WATCH THE PROGRAMS THAT COVER TOPICS IN DEPTH.

Watch the program that presents one guest for an hour, instead of a dozen for four minutes each. Watch the program that deals with only one subject in its hour, rather than four, eight, or twelve topics. Watch one good three-hour movie rather than three one-hour-long dramas.

Exercise: If you're going to watch television, at least do it with a little control. Get out that television guide, look through it like a menu, form a conscious decision about what you're going to put into your mind this week, and make sure that's the only time you turn on the set. Snacking on junk programs is as bad for your mind as potato chips are for your body.

WATCH PUBLIC TELEVISION.

Devote as much of your viewing schedule as possible to public television, which is slower-paced and contains more in-depth subject matter.

Exercise: Telephone your local public television station and ask how you can get a guide to their programming. Then send for it, even if you have to become a member and/or make a donation. You'd spend more than that amount just to play tennis for one hour. Think of it as an investment in your mind.

Exercise: Watch at least one program on public television every two weeks, no matter what it is. And, if you're not familiar with public television, you're in for a very pleasant surprise.

TURN OFF THE TV SET.

Unless you are totally engrossed in what you're watching, turn the set off and use the time for a project of your own. Don't waste one single precious minute of your life on mindless entertainment for its own sake; if you're not enjoying it, reclaim that time for your own use.

Exercise: Don't half-watch. Keep something interesting to do near the "off" button or by your remote control, and grab it as soon as your interest wanes or you recognize that what you're watching isn't worth your time. Better yet, get out of the house with someone else who is *also* half-watching! It will do the two of you good.

Do these at work:

DON'T DRINK OR EAT AT YOUR DESK.

An innocent cup of coffee, with or without a Danish, is often your subconscious way of breaking the tension of concentrating and attending properly to the job at hand. You will need to learn to accept this minor job-related stress if you want a strong attention span.

Exercise: Block off a period of two hours each day for the next two weeks, during which time you will eat or drink nothing while working. For the following two weeks, block off three hours.

DON'T TIE A BREAK TO THE CLOCK.

Instead, reward yourself with a break only at the completion of a task and before beginning another task. Don't let belly-rumbles govern your ability to function. Who's your boss, your stomach or your brain? (If it's your stomach, then you *really* need this chapter of *Brain Power*!)

Exercise: Make the deliberate decision to have a cup of coffee or take a brief break when you have *finished* a good-sized task. That way, you'll make it more difficult to allow yourself to take additional breaks during tasks.

WORK ON ONE TASK AT A TIME.

Finish one job before you begin the next. If you say you work better when you do three or four jobs at once, you probably have a short attention span and merely *feel* better grasshopping from task to task. You are losing not only time, but efficiency. Every time you drop something and pick up something else, you have to backtrack to see where you left off. This creates unnecessary overlaps of working time; it also has the potential for creating confusion. You are neither chimp nor child; learn to ignore the distractions, however tempting, of other jobs. Whatever it is, you'll get to it when you finish this one. Put a set of mental blinders on, and keep your eyes turned only to the work at hand.

Exercise: If possible, ask the people you work with not to interrupt you with any new task during the time they see you working on something else (unless it can't wait). Tasks are far harder to finish than they are to start.

DELEGATE RESPONSIBILITY.

Assign as many little chores to others as you can. This will free up larger blocks of time for larger projects. Too often, people keep hold of trivial tasks, sprinkling them through the workday just in order to *avoid*—no doubt subconsciously—attaining the very block of time they complain they can never find. Avoiding large blocks of time is another red-light indication of trouble with the attention span.

Exercise: When at work, make a list of all the calls you make and the letters you write that you don't really need to

144

do yourself. When at home, make a list of all the things you do *for* the kids that can be done *by* the kids. Study that list. Do you really want to or have the time to continue doing all this?

DO ALL THE LITTLE THINGS AT ONCE.

If you have nobody to whom you can delegate those small tasks, string them all together and do them in sequence instead of breaking up your workday with them.

Exercise: Today, instead of doing all those little chores now and then and here and there, write them down on a list instead. Then get on with the more important things. When the list has about ten little tasks on it, consider them as one big task and do them all at once.

LEARN HOW TO PREPARE.

You can do this either at home or at work. Assemble everything you will need to complete the task before you begin it. A short attention span will cause you to interrupt the job at hand to hop up frequently to fetch a reference book or a pair of scissors. Don't let it. Think the job through, and put together everything you will need to keep on working with no loss of concentration.

Exercise: Pick a convenient time—either at your workplace or in your home—to do one task of reasonable size that you've been intending to complete but "haven't got around to yet." Write down everything you need to accomplish that goal. Then, get it all together at the same time. For example, if you're writing a report, get out not only enough paper and an appropriate cover, get out all your reference sources, too. In other words, have *everything* handy. After awhile, this should become second nature, and whenever you sit down to work, you'll actually be able to work.

FINISH AN OLD PROJECT.

Exercise: Look around at home or at work, grab up the easiest abandoned project you can find, and finish it. It needn't be an important one. All it really needs to be is incomplete. Let's say you bought new buttons for an old winter coat, but haven't got around to doing it yet. Or let's say you bought a new package of Rolodex cards to bring your address file up to date. Do it now. Don't worry about other unfinished projects; as an exercise, select one, and only one, and finish it.

Exercise: Go now and throw out all the old stuff in the refrigerator and the stale stuff in your kitchen cabinets. It's easy, it's fun, and it's a good way to get started doing something constructive.

MAKE IT IMPOSSIBLE NOT TO COMPLETE A TASK.

Exercise: Remember that old winter coat needing the new buttons? Go and get it, take your scissors, and cut off all the old ones. You won't be able to wear the coat until the new ones are sewn on. If it's not the winter coat, look in the closet until you find a garment needing buttons or a hem or the stitching of a seam, and do it right away.

Now that you have practiced lengthening your attention span, you will find that one of the most significant results is that you will be more *capable* of finishing projects and therefore more *likely* to complete them. Making it hard *not* to complete the job makes it easier to tackle and finish it.

BRAIN BUILDER #75

FINISH WHAT YOU START.

Promise yourself to finish every worthwhile project you begin. This is not one of those New Year's resolutions to make January 1 and break January 2. If you actually swear to finish everything you start and take your promise seriously, you will take on fewer projects, thereby finding yourself with more time to finish what you *do* undertake. Ten finished projects are far more significant in your intellectual development than fifty projects merely begun.

There's a paradoxical corollary to the above paragraph: 1) Finish the project no matter how bad a job you think you're doing. 2) Don't be compulsive about finishing it.

The paradox is resolved this way. When you have completed enough unfinished jobs of increasing difficulty, taking increasing lengths of time to feel more confident in your attention span, perhaps half a dozen, you must take on projects that are truly worthy of your time; *but you should feel free to drop them the moment they cease to be worthwhile or the moment you discover you were wrong.*

In other words, you must drop a project only when and if the project becomes inadequate, not when and if *you* become inadequate. Thus, dropping a project becomes a conscious decision, not an unconscious way of wasting time. Don't rationalize! Be totally honest with yourself, and weigh the pros and cons objectively. If the negatives are heavier than the positives, don't throw good time after bad.

Exercise: Look around the house. Find any partly-done project and follow either one of these two alternatives: finish it or throw it out. Either way, you'll feel better afterward.

SLEEP LESS.

Unless you're so tired that you're sure you'll fall asleep within five minutes after your head hits the pillow, don't go to bed. Why should you? And if you don't go to sleep right away, get back up. For many people, sleep has less to do with rest than with being a good excuse for interrupting an activity. Sleep is the perfect escape, even better than television; it's an effective way to stop work on a project, stop an argument, or even stop living in the real world for a few hours.

Let's say you begin working on a project in the evening; perhaps you're refinishing a table, balancing your checkbook, looking over some office papers, or reading a book. If you take yourself off to bed before you're actually sleepy, then you're not physically tired. You're simply tired of the project. Unless you make a conscious decision to abandon it as not worth any more of your time—ever!—then continue with it. Abandoning it is bad for your attention span, bad for your powers of concentration, and that, in turn, affects your memory.

Exercise: If you're having a problem with sleeping too much at night, put away as many of your clocks as possible, or, for the next two weeks, turn them around so you can't see the time. It's amazing how just knowing that it's a particular evening hour can make you sleepy. Then, set your alarm to the time you'd *like* to go to sleep, and don't get into bed until the alarm rings. When you're accustomed to sleeping less, you can turn your clocks around to face you again.

DON'T EAT UNLESS YOU'RE HUNGRY.

Just like sleeping, eating has become a way of interrupting the day or the concentrated flow of what you're doing. Many managers of top corporations skip lunch entirely, unless it's strictly for business. They sleep fewer hours a night, too. We don't advocate skipping meals entirely, just cutting down on the time they "eat up," and eating only enough for genuine nourishment. Lunch for a working person should serve at least one of three purposes—nourishment, relaxation and enjoyment with friends or family, or a chance to meet business contacts. Otherwise, you'd be far better off staying at your desk until the appointed task is completed, taking a late "lunch" in which you take a stroll around a far less crowded city, or saving your appetite for dinner.

Dinner, too, should serve a purpose. Probably the most important purpose is meeting with family around the table to catch up on one another's day; joining a friend for a social evening either out or at home is also beneficial. But if you don't need the nourishment, then there's nothing wrong with skipping a full dinner and putting that time to better use in completing something requiring your attention. Contrary to what we were taught as children, mealtimes are not sacred occasions or ironclad obligations. They are merely habits and therefore breakable.

Exercise: For the next week, vary the time you eat your lunch or dinner in order to break the habit of expecting food at a certain time whether you need it or not.

BRAIN BUILDER #78

DON'T "SLEEP ON" A PROBLEM.

If you've got a tough one to crack, stay up for a little while longer and concentrate on its solution. As long as your body and brain are not actually crying out for sleep, stay with the problem; it's a wonderful feeling to see it crack before you do!

Increasing your attention span will clear out any remaining cobwebs from your brain and give you a feeling of intense energy and confidence. Just knowing that you *can* get the job done is half the work of the job itself!

Exercise: For the next two weeks, vary the hour that you go to bed at night. This is intended to break the habit of having to be in bed at a certain time or being incapable of functioning if you stay up any later. Then, if you stay up to deal with a problem instead of "sleeping on" it, your body will be ready.

Develop Your Senses and Learn to Trust Them

Remember our Kalahari bushman? He is a man whose well-developed senses can be trusted to keep him safe in his environment. All day every day, he exercises his senses of sight, smell, taste, touch, and hearing to bring him news of the world around him, news essential to his survival. He's developed his senses over the years, using instinct, intuition, insight, and experience. Our artist has developed her aesthetic sense—mostly of sight—through her inner instinct and outer experience as well.

Developing your senses and learning to trust them is an essential part of Brain Building. To single each sense out, develop it to its maximum potential, and analyze the information it brings you is an experience that will broaden and deepen your perceptions and encourage you to experience things more fully.

BRAIN BUILDER #79

FEAST YOUR SENSES AS MUCH AS POSSIBLE.

We told you that Brain Building would be fun, and this exercise is probably the most enjoyable of all in its appeal to the senses as well as to the intellect. The more often you do it, and the longer you take completing it, the sharper your senses will become. But urging is unnecessary here, and once a week will do.

Exercise: First, select a quiet evening for this exercise, a relaxed time when no deadlines confront you and nothing unpleasant or urgent is pressing. You might choose the evening of a stress-filled day because this is a totally relaxing exercise. Next make a trip to your favorite market and choose a group of *eye-appealing* and *fragrant* items for your dinner, food that does not have to be prepared but can be eaten raw. Include fresh fruits, vegetables, and bread, but not soft, pre-packaged bread. A crusty loaf, such as French or Italian bread, is best. Add cheese, if you like it, but make it a cheese with some zest and aroma—like Stilton or goat cheese—not artificially colored cheese-food cheese slices.

All this food must share these important ingredients: freshness, texture, color, and fragrance, but they should also contrast with one another in all the above details.

Now add a bunch of fresh flowers to your shopping cart, a mixed bunch of blooms, if possible. Flowers are in season all year—you don't have to purchase expensive roses when any fragrant blooms will do. Even in winter you can find a bunch of carnations in most markets.

Take all this good stuff home and lay it out on your table. Sit down and relax.

Now for the most important and most enjoyable part of the exercise: developing each sense in turn.

1) **Sight:** Pick up each item individually and look at it. Take your time; use your eyes alone to explore the wonder of its shape and size and color. Look at it as though you've never seen it before, as though you or it had just arrived from Mars. Let each item fill your eyes with its uniqueness.

2) **Touch:** Now for the textures. Pay each item solemn attention with your fingers, focusing on your sense of touch alone. Dim the lights, if possible, or shut your eyes. *Feel* the bread's crust; then break a piece off and let your fingers explore the loaf's interior. Let your fingers give you the contrast between the sleek skin of an apple and the fluffiness of the flowers and the oiliness of the butter. Hold an orange or a lemon in your hand and explore the scaly indentations of its rind. How does an orange differ in feel from a ripe avocado? Pick out a flower and hold it first against your cheek, then to your lips. Do the same thing with a different flower. Ask your sense of touch to give you as much information as possible.

3) **Smell:** Now pick up every item in turn and smell it, beginning with the more subtle aromas and leading up to the flowers and the cheese. Again, take your time; allow the occasion to be a pleasure as well as a lesson. This is a sensual intellectual experience; make the most if it. Whether smelling flowers or herbs, smell the stems as well as the blooms or leaves. Linger with each aroma until you have absorbed it into your sense of smell and think you might recognize it again.

4) **Hearing:** With your eyes still shut, listen to the crackling sound the bread crust makes as you tear a piece off the loaf. Break off a rib of celery and hear how the stringy part sounds as it separates from the flesh. Pull a section of the orange away from the skin and listen to the juice welling out and dripping onto the plate. As you take each bite of the various foods, listen to the sounds your teeth make in con-

tact with them, the crunch of the raw vegetables and the tearing sound of the herbs.

5) **Taste:** Indulge your sense of taste and sharpen it by concentrating on one flavor at a time. Take each item in turn, and don't mix flavors in any one bite. Try a little bread, then a vegetable, then fruit, and then maybe the bread again. Think of the components of each flavor; try to separate and identify them: the yeastiness of the bread. Is there sugar in it? Can you taste the salt? The fruit—is it more sweet than acid or the other way around? Chew each bite thoroughly before you swallow; eat slowly. Take a sip of water between bites to refresh your palate. Touch a flower to your tongue; then follow it by just the lightest lick of creamery butter.

Brief Quiz

A QUIZ FOR THE END OF WEEK SEVEN

1) Is intellectual growth hopeless without expanding attention span?
2) Which is the television channel to watch?
3) Which is the radio station to listen to?
4) When should you drop a project?
5) Will it hurt you to sleep a little less?
6) Will it hurt you to eat a little less?
7) What were the senses suggested to use while eating?
8) Do you remember any of the sentences you read in the "sentence memory" section?
9) Do you remember any of the salient points of the passages?
10) Do you remember any of the names of the people quoted?

ANSWERS

1) Sorry, yes.
2) Public television.
3) Public radio. (Not a tough question, was it?)
4) When it becomes inadequate, not when you do.
5) Assuming you're not ill, no.
6) Assuming you're not ill, no.
7) All five of them.
8) If not, go back and read them again.
9) If not, go back and read them again.
10) If not, go back and read them again.

CHAPTER

11

WEEK EIGHT

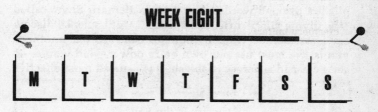

| M | T | W | T | F | S | S |

Building Communication

TOOLS YOU WILL NEED FOR WEEK EIGHT:
A small tape recorder and a little humility. If you can't lay
your hands on the humility right away, cheer up. Most of us
hide it so well that we can't find it when we need it.

"Speech is a mirror of the soul: as a man speaks, so he is."

—Publilius Syrus

Whether it's accomplished by speaking, drawing, writing,
music, an expressive silence, a pregnant pause, the lift of
an eyebrow, a sympathetic smile, or the technology of satellites, communication is the *science* and, even more, the
art of transmitting and imparting information from one
mind to another.

By means of music, we can set a mood, evoke emotions,
stimulate feelings of romance, sadness, suspense, dread, or

exhilaration. By the mute but eloquent clasp of a hand, we can communicate our feelings of warmth and empathy. Our artist communicates her thoughts with her brush; to our stockbroker, a run of numbers across his computer screen may tell him everything he needs to know. Even a primitive man like our Kalahari bushman can communicate to others of his tribe, who cannot read or write, by drawing with a stick on the ground—a zebra, two zebra, many zebra, in the place where the big rocks are.

But, common to most of us, communication is accomplished through words, what George Bernard Shaw called "the divine gift of articulate speech." Until science discovers some method whereby humans can read one another's minds, we must use our own brain power—and words—to get a clear idea across in the shortest, surest, most effective way.

Clarity Is the Key

A clear idea. The key element in any form of communication is *clarity*. Fuzzy thinking and fuzzy expression are the sure signs of a lazy brain operating at less than full power. On the other hand, clarity of thinking and clarity of communication are two sides of the same golden coin, and the development of both is paramount in building your brain.

Having to get an idea across to others forces you to put your own thoughts in order. Whether you are guiding a friend, managing employees, or holding down a challenging job, your effectiveness depends largely on how clearly you can make known your needs and instructions, how easily and fully you can make others comprehend. To do this, you must first be able to organize your own thinking into a logical and easily-communicated structure.

In a more leisurely age, before the word "communication" was a media buzzword, grammar schools, high schools, and colleges placed a high premium on developing the skill of presenting thoughts in order. The exercise was called the essay or the composition or even, "What I Did on My Summer Vacation." Remember how you were graded up or down on your clarity of expression? That clarity is a skill that can still be learned.

Learn to Communicate First with Yourself

BRAIN BUILDER #80

THINK BEFORE YOU SPEAK.

Don't leap into any discussion from a standing start. Take a moment to put your thoughts into a rough order, at least. What is it you are trying to impart? An impression? A fact or set of facts? An emotion? A moral? An anecdote? What do you hope to provoke in your listener? Surprise? Laughter? Indignation? A good argument? Support for your position? Which of the words bubbling on your lips will have the best chance of securing that effect? Which statements to follow will bolster the first, lending weight to your position?

Exercise: The next time you're having a conversation about a significant subject—politics, religion, national defense, economics—pause for a few minutes and compel yourself to think first every time you begin to speak.

BRAIN BUILDER #81

LISTEN TO WHAT YOU SAY.

Try to judge your speaking from another person's viewpoint. Use your speaking as a means to organize your thinking as well as vice versa. What if one of the others taking part in this conversation, discussion, or debate, had voiced these same thoughts in the same manner and the same words? Would you be swayed? Convinced?

Exercise: The next time you're really angry about something, pick up the tape recorder and blast into it everything

155

that's on your mind. Don't play it back for three days. If you do this every time you're angry for the period of a month or more, playing the tape back three days later, you'll really gain some perspective on yourself.

The important thing to bear in mind is this: when you hear your anger after it's cooled, and when you listen to your own voice speaking rash and injudicious words, you will very likely be horrified and embarrassed. *Is that me?* you might wonder. Imagine now that somebody else was listening to the tape and forming a judgment about you on the strength of it.

BRAIN BUILDER #82

MEAN WHAT YOU SAY.

After a heated discussion in which you've taken part, select from all your rhetoric the six most important things you said. Write them down. Then, against each statement, list what you actually meant privately. Do the two columns match? How many times did your thoughts concur with your statements? If all six match, then good for you. If not, begin to practice stating your meaning, not what you think will prove the other person wrong. Clear communication is predicated on speaking the truth, not on verbal wrestling matches.

Exercise: Any time during the next month that you have an argument, resolve not to say anything during the argument that you don't actually believe is true or that you don't actually feel. Don't say anything to your opponent *to persuade him to your viewpoint.* The point here is to rely strictly on the facts. If this should cost you the argument, then very possibly the other person is right!

Saying only what you really mean in an argument will win you friends. People who say things they don't mean will be called manipulative, and with good reason.

BRAIN BUILDER #83

LEARN TO RECOGNIZE WHAT OTHERS MEAN
DESPITE WHAT THEY SAY.

You must realize that others are doing the same—speaking to persuade. If you merely go by what others say, you will often be misled. What others say to us may differ radically from what they mean, depending on what they want us to believe or how they want us to behave.

The most obvious example is that of a campaigning politician who wants our votes, and will promise whatever it takes to gain them. This is perhaps democracy's greatest weakness: that the public good, long- or short-term, is frequently only a secondary consideration, if it is a consideration at all. Your boss may tell you only what he thinks will benefit some plan of action; a co-worker with his own promotion in mind may tell you what he thinks will make you fail; your wife, afraid of losing you, may say whatever she feels will bind you to the children and thus the marriage; your parents, reluctant to relinquish their control over your life, may say things to make you lack confidence in yourself; your children, enjoying the good life at your expense, may tell you anything that will make you feel guilty if you don't go on giving them what they want.

Everybody pulls your strings. Everybody wants to project his or her personal mental picture inside your head. Right now, you are very likely a jigsaw puzzle composed of pieces that other people have fashioned. So, in the face of all this manipulation, who are you to believe?

You must believe in yourself. But do you? Try this set of exercises to find out:

Exercise: When you have an original idea to impart, do you preface it with "I read . . ." in order to get your listener to take you more seriously? Are you always quoting others? Are you frequently silent because you feel you have nothing worthwhile to contribute? Do you hesitate to voice a comment until you can offer authoritative "proof"? Most great thinkers don't have proof based on some "higher authority." If you can answer yes to two or more of the above four questions, you need to work as hard on building your self-confidence as you do on building your intelligence.

BRAIN BUILDER #84

LEARN TO CUT FROM THE BOTTOM.

All your life you've heard that the lead sentence of any good newspaper story should contain "who, what, where, when, how, why." It's true. What's more, anything written for a newspaper is cut from the bottom up for length. The first paragraph is the most important, the second paragraph is next in importance, and so on down the line, with the editor literally cutting off the paragraphs *from the bottom* up to make the story fit. Editors used to perform this task with an actual pair of scissors; today, they can merely touch the "delete" button on a word processor keyboard.

One method of learning to communicate directly is editing yourself—cutting from the bottom, as it were. If you have one hour to get your point across, you probably could say everything you want to in that time. An hour on one topic seems like forever to a speaker. But suppose you have only thirty minutes? Or thirty seconds?

Exercise: Suppose you have only thirty seconds to give your side of a burning issue of the day. What would you say first? Second? Third? Time's up. Did you get your point across? Did you communicate successfully? If not, practice this exercise.

BRAIN BUILDER #85

PRACTICE CONCISE COMMUNICATING.

Exercise: Try describing the following text in fewer than fifty words.

This is a truly challenging exercise. In how brief a span of time, with how few words and phrases, can you get your point across with maximum clarity? I know children who communicate perfectly in one word: "MINE!" or "NO!" But here, at the crunch, is where, with a little effort, you can really build a precision of language that communicates. However, don't get carried away, like Simple Simon in the old joke who put up a sign over his store reading "Fresh Fish Sold Here."

His friend Sam objected. "Why 'Here'? You don't need that word. Where else would you be selling fish?" So Simon took his brush and painted out "Here."

"Why 'Sold' "? grumbled Sam. "You don't need 'Sold.' Who would imagine you're *giving* fish away?" Out went "Sold."

"Why 'Fresh?' Nobody expects you to be selling *spoiled* fish. Take out 'Fresh.' " Simon obliged, and the sign read simply "Fish."

"*Now* is that good enough for you?" demanded Simple Simon.

Sam shook his head. "My *nose* already told me 'Fish'."

In a way, Sam was right. The sign probably wasn't necessary at all, at least when the wind was blowing in the right direction. The pervasive perfume of fish was a form of communication in itself.

And now you see the limitations of this overly concise kind of communication.

We aren't simpletons, and we aren't selling fish in a high wind; we must use words as tools to get our ideas from one brain into another. If you sharpen your tools and keep them well-honed, you'll be able to use them effectively in a minimum of time.

As you know, I'm not a fan of capsule news briefs or "instant" television communication, or in fact anything that denies you the chance to consider an important subject in the depth and detail it deserves. The idea behind the above Brain Builder is not to train you to communicate in twenty-five words or less, but to train you to select the most important point you're trying to make automatically, and to home in on it in a limited time frame. You are learning how to set your thoughts in order, to make the expression of those thoughts more effective. *But these are only exercises, remember, not real communication.*

Communicating Through Speaking with Others

COMMUNICATE POSITIVELY.

It's much easier to communicate when you don't worry about what your listeners think of you. Good communicators are well loved. An excellent example is that of former President Ronald Reagan, whom the press immediately nicknamed "The Great Communicator." Until the Iran-Contra hearings, and probably again shortly afterward, President Reagan was the all-time most popular President of the United States. Politics aside, his delivery was brilliant—short words, brief, direct sentences spoken with feeling, accompanied by an earnest look straight into the camera lens and the public eye. In his long career, President Reagan had learned many basic skills of good communicating, including showing the positive side of every topic.

Exercise: The next dozen times you need to talk to someone, say something nice first and take note of how they react.

Exercise: Start communicating in a positive sense whenever you can, without stretching the truth or distorting it and without telling lies. Tell the truth, but *good* truth! For example, sit down across the kitchen table from one of your least-appreciated friends and personally explain to him or her what you think makes him a good (even great) person and why. Positive communication makes everyone feel better; negative communication makes everybody feel worse.

As you gain practice in communicating positively, it is likely that people will begin to like you more and more. Then, when you have a *bad* truth to impart, you will do it more easily and gain far more acceptance for it. Your listeners may even make a special effort to correct the problem.

BRAIN BUILDER #87

DO ALL YOUR IMPORTANT COMMUNICATING YOURSELF.

Don't delegate to others the most important things you want to get across to somebody. The more practice you get, the better a communicator you will become, and the less you will fear the consequences of poor communication. Making a few mistakes at first is far better for brain building than a lifetime spent using others as mediators. No matter how good these mediators may be, they cannot possibly make your thoughts, ideas, and instructions as clear as you can. Accept the results of any mistakes as a major part of the learning process. It's the same as falling off a bike: eventually you become an expert rider.

BRAIN BUILDER #88

PUT YOUR WORDS IN CONTEXT.

Make certain your words have the correct context and that the context is communicated to your listeners. One of the major reasons for misunderstanding is that something or everything one says is taken out of its proper context. To further understanding, make certain that your words are first established in a clear, succinct context that can't be misinterpreted. The question, "Why don't you see a doctor about that?" can range in meaning from a suggestion to an accusation!

Exercise: For the next month, keep pen and paper next to the telephone, and make a note of every time the person on the other end of the line doesn't seem to understand what you just said. If possible, write down the misunderstood phrase or sentence, then lay it aside until the end of the week. At that time, reread the words and ask yourself whether you would have understood if someone had said the same thing to you. In other words, don't leave too much information inside your head. Remember, the other person cannot possibly know what's in your head, and your words must explain it well, or your listener won't understand.

161

BECOME AWARE OF YOUR LISTENERS.

Be aware of how many and who they are. Notice that you will speak differently to three people from how you will speak to one, even on the same subject. People who do a lot of public speaking to large audiences are often unable to talk to a single person on a one-to-one basis; they "address" them instead of simply holding a conversation. If you have identified this as your problem—that you address different people differently in different situations—practice to correct it except in cases where you choose to do it deliberately. But learn to tell the difference.

Exercise: The next time you visit your mother, try to talk to her as you would to a dear friend who is not your mother. If you find this at all difficult—or even impossible—you'll see just how much you're altering what you're saying and obscuring the path of real communication.

PUT YOURSELF IN THE OTHER PERSON'S PLACE.

As he or she is speaking, put yourself in the other person's place. If you do this correctly, it can be most illuminating. Don't hesitate to cross "barriers" of age, race, and gender. Imagine yourself to be the other person speaking—black if you're white, white if you're black, old, young, male, female, a parent, a grandparent, a boss, an employee, a friend. Understanding why people think as they do might be a big jolt to your objectivity. You might find yourself agreeing with—*communicating* with—someone you never saw eye-to-eye with before this.

If you are trying to communicate with somebody who isn't intellectually inclined, don't speak to his brain; try speaking to his personality instead. It's the personality—set of values, background, upbringing, gender, race, and other factors—that is creating a barrier between you. You must deal with it. If you do, you'll have a lot more success communicating with the intellect behind the personality.

Exercise: Have a discussion with a friend in which the two of you take the parts of people who are different from either one of you. If you're both white, try on a black person's shoes. If you're female, try on male shoes, and so on.

BRAIN BUILDER #91

NEVER TRY TO EXPLAIN A SUBJECT WHEN YOU DON'T
KNOW ENOUGH ABOUT IT.

Teaching something is a great way to learn it, but don't waste your own or anyone else's time by teaching something you don't know in depth. When a friend comes to you for information or help, take the time to read up on the subject so that you don't impart any misinformation. Then, untangle your thoughts and set them in order, and you will communicate effectively to your and your friend's benefit.

Exercise: If you are still in school, you might offer to tutor a classmate who needs help in an area that you comprehend much better than he does.

Exercise: If you are being promoted at work, imagine how you would teach your job to your replacement. (Try not to imagine how you'd do this if you were fired.)

BRAIN BUILDER #92

TRY NOT TO USE THE TELEPHONE AS A MEANS OF COMMUNICATION.

The telephone, which ought to be used as a convenience, has, unfortunately, become the chief form of communication for too many people, replacing the written word and the face-to-face meeting. That's too bad, because it's almost impossible to make real contact over a telephone. When you can see the person you're talking to, you can gauge his understanding in a hundred subtle ways, including his body language and facial expression. When you write a letter, you have the benefit of the revision process; you can make sure that you are expressing yourself exactly as you wish. Over the telephone, you give up both benefits—you can't see the other person's expression; neither can you revise. In person, the emphasis is placed on the other; in writing, it's placed on you. But there is no real emphasis on anybody in a phone conversation, so keep your calls short, to the point, and informational.

Exercise: If there is anybody living in your town or city with whom you talk over the telephone for more than an hour a week, stop all the calls. Instead, *see* this person for the same amount of time. For example, if you usually talk for an hour, have a Saturday morning one-hour breakfast visit. If it's two hours, make it lunch.

BRAIN BUILDER #93

STOP USING THE WORD "OPINION."

Opinions aren't sacred. In fact, the word "opinion" is often used to mask or glorify a dumb idea. And all opinions aren't equal. Many of them are just plain wrong. "I have a right to my opinion" frequently means "I don't know how to justify what I just said with facts." In other words, a tightly-held opinion is the hallmark of a mind closed just as tightly. Open your mind and let out those stale opinions.

There's room, of course, for honest disagreement. But bear in mind that when you deal with opinions, unless you are dealing with simple basic likes and dislikes, such as "I like chocolate" or "I don't like chocolate," you are not dealing with facts or truth.

Truth is absolute; opinion is relative. There is only one truth, even though it may be described in many different correct ways, like the six blind men who felt the different parts of an elephant with their fingertips and described it as a wall, a snake, a rope, and so on. Take a mountain: It can be described from above, from below, from any angle, from a historical perspective according to who lived there, from a botanical perspective according to what grew there, from a zoological perspective according to the mountain's wildlife, from a topographical or meteorological or a geological perspective, but the truth of the mountain itself is undeniably absolute.

Exercise: For the next two weeks, don't try to stop using the word "opinion." Instead, make a mark on a piece of paper every time you use it or would have been inclined to use it if you hadn't read this first. This will tell you whether you have this "opinion" problem—nearly everyone does—and gauge the depth of it.

Exercise: After two weeks, stop using the word "opinion" entirely and see how this forces you to defend your position with information. And if you're stuck talking with someone who tries to use his "opinion" against you, say something like, "That's an interesting opinion. How do you support it?"

Words That Carry a Hidden Agenda

Before we go on to our next Brain Builder, let's stop for a minute to think about the difference between "denotative" and "connotative" words. Basically, a denotative word is one that describes something in the plainest, most matter-of-fact way, with no additional meaning. A connotative word bears a suggestion or implication of something beyond the mere description, a word that has a hidden agenda, if you will. Simply put, a denotative word is objective, while a connotative word is subjective.

Let's take a few examples: "Her nail polish was red." "Her nail polish was blood-red." In those sentences, the simple word "red" is a denotative word; "blood-red" is connotative. "Blood-red" seems to imply that the woman is glamorous, high-living, daring, perhaps a little "loose" with her attentions. "Hardworking" is denotative; "workaholic" is connotative. "Rural" is denotative, and so is "country," but "homespun" and "hick" are connotative—one suggests everything cozy; the other suggests everything backward.

BRAIN BUILDER #94

USE MORE DENOTATIVE WORDS.

Denotative words express thoughts; connotative words express opinions. Connotative words are often loaded; you'll find them in slanted newspaper stories and in the speech of anybody trying to persuade or stir the emotions. For example, using "Reagan's economic policies" is better than using "Reaganomics." The former forces you to explain what you feel. The latter is merely name-calling. And name-calling only makes *you* look bad.

Exercise: The next few times you find yourself using a great many connotative words in an argument, take some quiet time to take a look at your thoughts on the subject at issue. Using an excess of connotative words this way often means that you don't actually know anything *denotatively* negative to say. If that's the case, maybe you shouldn't be arguing this topic at all.

I've often thought that if people only knew the facts beforehand, most arguments wouldn't even take place.

Exercise: Gather together a few different newspapers—not the same newspaper from different days—and look through the editorial section of each one, picking out editorials that use a great many connotative instead of denotative words and editorials that use denotative instead of connotative words. Compare the two. As you take note that the heavily connotative language is a great deal less convincing than the heavily denotative language, keep in mind that you yourself appear more or less convincing to others depending on the language you use.

Exercise: The following is a list of connotative words that you hear in everyday life. Do you know their objective (denotative) counterparts? The answers will follow.

1) Star Wars	8) Angel of Death
2) cop	9) put to sleep
3) Prince Charles	10) oil-rich
4) women's libber	11) lady
5) convict	12) gentleman
6) Mother Nature	13) bankrolled
7) Father Time	14) tells stories

Answers

1) Strategic Defense Initiative	8) death
2) police officer	9) killed
3) Charles Windsor	10) oil-producing
4) feminist	11) woman
5) prisoner	12) man
6) nature	13) financed
7) time	14) lies

LEARN TO ADMIT YOUR ERRORS.

Don't ever be afraid to be wrong; this fear will hold back your intellectual development. It's almost impossible to see your flaws in communication unless you are communicating with others who will point them out or question your statements closely. Respond openly, not defensively, to the challenges. This is perhaps the best opportunity you'll get to discover your errors and correct them. If you can't get used to admitting your mistakes, it's unlikely you'll ever get beyond them. Admit you're wrong, and embrace the truth gladly. From this you will grow wiser and wiser. Central to your intellectual growth is changing beliefs you've discovered to be wrong. Clinging to your old errors will just waste your precious time and energy and will never make you right.

Exercise: At least once a day for the next week, say *aloud*, "I was wrong," when you find yourself in error. If you're alone, say it the moment you discover it. If you are with others, wait until you're alone and *then* say it aloud. The following week, do it twice a day. After a month of this, you should be getting used to the fact that you're routinely wrong about things and that it's perfectly normal. Now the exercise starts getting tough. For the two weeks following that, say "I was wrong" aloud once a day even if you're not alone, unless there's a good reason not to. Then, for two more weeks, go the full limit. Every time you find out you were wrong and somebody else was right, even about something minor, *admit to that person that you were wrong.* (Remember, they probably know it already.)

DON'T DEFEND YOUR POINT OF VIEW AGAINST EVERY CRITICISM.

Most points of view have bad aspects as well as good ones. That doesn't necessarily mean that you've made the wrong choice. But if you knock yourself out trying to prove to a critical listener that you're right on every point that's been attacked, and if you're proved wrong, then the rest of your argument will tend to lose its credibility, especially in the areas where your listener doesn't quite understand you. He or she will assume, even if only subconsciously, that if your argument is weak or exaggerated in obvious areas, it will be weak or exaggerated in less-obvious areas, too. In the same way, learn that exaggeration doesn't strengthen an argument; rather, it weakens it by reducing the credibility of the speaker.

Exercise: At least once a week from now on, each and every time someone catches a weakness in your argument that you *know* is a weakness, admit it. Say, "Yes, that *does* appear to be a weakness." Your argument will gain strength from your added credibility because your listeners will soon learn that you will acknowledge weaknesses where you see them. This will make them feel that when you don't acknowledge weaknesses, there may actually be none!

BRAIN BUILDER #97

Don't raise your voice.

Don't shout, argue, threaten, or raise your voice for a month. Intimidation is for bullies; you communicate much more effectively when there isn't a hostile/defensive shield between you and your listener. If what you say has merit, communicating it calmly will be as effective—actually, *more* effective—than raising your voice. If your argument is without merit, no amount of yelling will make it stronger, and all you'll be communicating is defensiveness and anger, along with a staggering decibel level. Don't be like the American tourist who thought he could make the French waiter understand by yelling his order more and more loudly.

Practice getting your ideas across quietly or not at all. If you really want to get somebody's attention, lower your voice, even to a whisper. You'll be surprised at how many people will strain to hear you, afraid of missing something important. If you can do this for one month, you will be able to do it forever.

DON'T TRY TO ENLIGHTEN UNWILLING PEOPLE.

In most cases, people don't wish to be all that edified, and certainly not by someone standing next to them, unless you possess top credentials in the field of discussion. Don't let it worry you. State your case as unemotionally and factually as you know how and in an organized way. If you persuade somebody, fine. If not, that's his problem, not yours. Ideally, discussions should enlighten both parties, no matter who is the more knowledgeable at the outset. Practically, however, discussions usually leave neither person any better off. Generally speaking, this is because most discussions are just two monologues going on at the same time. You can remedy this in your own case, at least, by using a discussion to enlighten you.

There is nearly always something to be gained by speaking with another person, even if it doesn't result in a change in point of view. If nothing else, you can see the consequences of a lack of knowledge or a lack of objectivity. If you're dealing with a subjective mentality, see how subjectivity destroys sound thinking and intellectual growth. Are there areas in which you are allowing subjectivity to cloud your *own* thinking?

Exercise: Make a short list of the people in your life who actually enlighten *you*. (I'll bet this is going to be *very* brief.)

LISTEN TO OTHERS.

Listen to the negatives as well as the positives and learn from both. If you want to communicate with and to others, a discussion is a great place to learn. In any discussion, look for these clues: where does the other person become illogical, where emotional? Are you doing the same without noticing it? How do you feel when the other person says "you're wrong"? Do you become angry? Defensive?

Exercise: The next time someone tells you you're wrong about something, don't say a word. Just listen. And listen carefully—she may be right. Pay particular attention to *how* people tell you you're wrong, and the effect their methods have on you. Remember that this will be the effect you'll have on others when you use those expressions yourself.

Objectivity is as important in communicating as clarity. Practice remaining objective no matter how hotly the argument threatens to escalate. Without objectivity, emotions can flood in to take the place of reason, and the discussion loses its intellectual value.

What about slang? If the other speaker used expressions like "no way" or "you've gotta be kidding," or "I don't buy that," were you insulted? Did you become angry? If only negatives resulted from the use of slang, remember to delete these phrases from your own vocabulary unless your intention is simply to provoke.

BRAIN BUILDER #100

DON'T BE ARGUMENTATIVE.

Watch yourself carefully so that you don't appear to be argumentative. People don't pay much attention to argumentative speakers. Nobody likes to be harangued. Many people manage to turn every discussion into an argument. Make sure you're not one of them.

Do most of the people you speak to seem argumentative to you? If so, there's a good chance the problem lies with you.

Exercise: Strike up conversations with people you know casually but to whom you have no emotional ties one way or another. Stay on neutral ground in your selection of topics; keep off the subjects of politics and religion or hot, loaded topics such as abortion. If they still seem quarrelsome or contentious in general, the argumentative one is almost certainly you.

Just because you're combative doesn't mean you're not right. You may be right; you may be brilliant; you may even be intellectual. But you're going to have a hard time convincing others, if you can get them to listen at all. You won't be communicating ideas; you'll be communicating a bad personality.

BRAIN BUILDER #101

TALK TO THOSE CLOSEST TO YOU.

In today's turbulent world, it isn't easy to express feelings in words. We are surrounded by artificial substitutes for real communication—saccharine greeting cards, mylar balloons that carry sentimental messages, acrylic plush bears wearing hearts, and bumper stickers proclaiming a sentimental attachment to a city, a pet, or a rifle association. Superficial relationships bring superficial communication. Don't carry on deep or confidential conversations with strangers. Talk instead with your mate or your closest friends. In intimate relationships, there is the potential for the greatest and most genuine communication.

Exercise: Once a week for the next several weeks, initiate and carry through a meaningful conversation of at least thirty minutes with a different member of your family or group of friends, starting with the easiest person to approach and ending with that eighteen-year-old boy or that ninety-year-old woman.

BRAIN BUILDER #102

STUDY ENGLISH.

You always hear somebody saying that he or she is planning to take a course in French or Italian or even Japanese. I'd say the casual study of a second language is a waste of time; the gain is less than the loss. I favor a gradual, natural transition to a universal language, and speaking in separate languages is contrary to that aim. If you want to spend the time to study a language, I suggest that Americans make a further study of English—its grammar, forms, and etymology, its poetry and prose, and the almost infinite variety of the stylists who have written in the tongue. English is one of the world's richest languages and, practically as well as aesthetically speaking, a better grasp of your own language will do you far more good than a halting grasp of Spanish, French, or something else.

Exercise: Buy a book about common speaking errors in English and read it. Pinpoint those errors you yourself make and become aware of when you make them so that you can eliminate these errors from your speech.

Communicating Through Writing

BRAIN BUILDER #103

KEEP A MEMOIR.

Keep a diary, journal, or memoir, and write in it at times you yourself determine. Because you're writing only for your own eyes and nobody else's judgment and because you're writing about those things you know best—the events of your own life—keeping a journal will help you to overcome hesitation about or inability to communicate by means of the written word. Don't feel obligated to write in your journal every day or even every week. And don't agonize over how good or bad your writing style is. Aim only for clarity in expressing what happened and how you felt about it. At the time, don't even reread what you've written.

On New Year's Eve of each year, take out your journal and reread the year gone by. How well did you communicate what happened? Does a rereading actually bring the event to life? Do your words evoke memories or are they lacking in detail, fact, accuracy, or feeling?

Exercise: If you would like to keep some sort of journal, but would rather not face the pressure of writing in it every day, use the following technique to break that "black or white" habit. Buy a looseleaf notebook to use as a journal, and write in it no more and no less frequently than once a week for the next year. I suggest for this exercise that you write no fewer than one page and no more than two. You're allowed no less than five minutes, but no more than thirty minutes to write each journal entry. And at the end of the year, you must remove and throw away no fewer than six and no more than twelve weeks' entries. This "editing" will help relieve the compulsion to write every day and will leave you with a good body of work that will equal a full-length book every five years.

Exercise: If you feel compulsive about writing every day or guilty about not writing at all, try this: for the next two weeks, write a daily "headline" about yourself, highlighting some event of the day. Just the headline will do; you needn't write an entire news story. It will look something like this:

SUNDAY   MIKE GOODFELLOW BUYS A NEW PAIR
                OF SHOES!
MONDAY   SUBWAY DOOR NEARLY CLOSES ON MIKE
                GOODFELLOW!
TUESDAY   MIKE GOODFELLOW FALLS IN LOVE!

After a couple of weeks, you'll come to see why there may be no need to write about yourself every day. After all, only one of the above three days was worth a journal entry. (And if you fall in love once every week, maybe none of the above are worth recording.)

BRAIN BUILDER #104

WRITE LETTERS.

Write to friends as well as pen pals you've never met. Writing to people you know very well will give you a chance to discuss more personal subjects in a way you can't do with outsiders. One of the greatest of the side benefits is that close communication with intimates enhances the sense of security and emotional well-being of everyone involved.

Exercise: Get started by going out and buying six colorful postcards of your own city and sending them to anyone out of town who would like to hear from you. It shouldn't be too painful to write only a paragraph, and you may even get a nice letter or two back.

WRITE TO PEN FRIENDS.

Exercise: Write a note to the embassy of a foreign country of your choice and ask them how to find a "pen pal" in their home country.

This will compel you to explain things about our country that you have always taken for granted and that you will now re-examine in the light of making them clear to another person. Explaining familiar political and social phenomena to a stranger provides you with an almost-pure opportunity to sharpen your powers of communication. And maybe gain a little perspective on our less-than-perfect country, as well.

WRITE CRITICAL LETTERS.

Without becoming personal or abusive, sit down and drop a line to the editors of newspapers and magazines, commenting objectively on what you dislike about their publications. Keep to the topic and present your arguments logically. You despise the *Sports Illustrated* swimsuit issue as sexist? Write them a letter and tell them why. It won't hurt them personally, and you'll get good practice in communicating. (Don't, however, expect them to take you so seriously that they drop the swimsuit issue; you'll never live that long.) Some publication may actually print your letter, and upon rereading it, you'll gain more perspective on your style.

Exercise: Once a month for the next year, write a letter to *someone*, no matter how short.

BRAIN BUILDER #107

READ THE LETTERS TO THE EDITOR IN THE NEWSPAPER.

This will help you see in what ways the writer succeeds or (more often) fails to communicate or convince. See where logic falls apart and emotion takes over; see how often faith is invoked where reason and logic are required. Don't bother to read the Letters columns in magazines, however, because they are not usually communication-oriented and are so heavily edited.

Exercise: Choose a letter with which you agree but which has failed to put the salient point across. Then write your own letter of the same length as the one printed. Send it to the newspaper yourself.

BRAIN BUILDER #108

CONDENSE EDITORIALS.

Exercise: Rewrite your newspaper's editorials or letters to the editor, condensing them into one paragraph. Choose a lively letter or editorial, and, taking its points in order of their importance, condense the gist of it into as few words as possible. Then show both the original and your condensation to a friend and ask if he or she gets the point of the piece from your abridged version. This is the corollary exercise to your expressing yourself verbally in as few words as possible and will strengthen not only your mental organization, but also enhance your powers of succinctness, a most valuable weapon in the intellectual arsenal.

BRAIN BUILDER #109

WRITE LETTERS TO STRANGERS.

Exercise: Remember what we said earlier about practicing positive communications? Write a complimentary letter to someone you've never met, but whom you admire. Explain exactly what it is you like about this person and why. Feel free to express your feelings, but don't get emotional; strive instead for objectivity. I recently wrote just such a letter to a fellow author whose work I respect.

Brief Quiz

AND HERE'S YOUR QUIZ FOR THE END OF WEEK EIGHT

1) What are the two key elements in any form of communication?
2) What's the best way to judge your communication skills?
3) What is the major cause of misunderstanding in communication?
4) Should you speak differently to different people?
5) Which is the worst for effective communication: the telephone, a letter, or a meeting?
6) Why should you stop using the word "opinion"?
7) Who said, "Truth is absolute; opinion is relative"?
8) What's the difference between a denotative word and a connotative word?
9) What language should you study?
10) What is the greatest enemy of effective communication?

ANSWERS

1) Clarity and objectivity.
2) From the viewpoint of others.
3) Words given or taken out of context.
4) Yes. You should suit *every* communication to the audience.
5) The telephone.
6) Because it'll force you to think.
7) I did.
8) A denotative word is objective; a connotative word is subjective.
9) English!
10) Emotion.

WEEK NINE

| M | T | W | T | F | S | S |

Building Information

TOOLS YOU WILL NEED FOR WEEK NINE:
At least two different daily newspapers.

"Remember Bacon's recommendation to the reader: 'Read not to contradict and confute; nor to believe and take for granted; nor to find talk and discourse; but to weigh and consider.' "

—Mortimer J. Adler and Charles Van Doren,
How to Read a Book

If we accept the computer as a metaphor for the brain itself, then the intellect is the hardware and information the software. A computer accepts all information impartially, sorts it without judging it, stores it, and regurgitates it on command. But a computer chip is built to last practically forever while human beings are comparatively short-lived. All information is *not* of equal value; if we had eternity to sift through the information of previous centuries—all the books, music, art, ideas generated by the human race, all the wonders of the universe known and unknown—we could take our time selecting the best and leaving the rest.

And that's dealing only with the intellectual heritage of the past. In the present we are cannonaded by information from every possible source; there are media available today that our parents only dreamed of—or had nightmares about! Two thousand eight hundred years ago, the news that the Greek army had finally conquered Troy was relayed to the mainland of Greece by a series of huge signal fires set along the mountain ridges on the western coast of Asia Minor. One by one, the torches lit up the sky, carrying news of the victory from one beacon fire to the next until their glow could be seen on the eastern shore of Hellas. The details of the war itself had to wait until the warriors returned, but the fires told the most important part of the story. And what a way to write a headline: in flames! More than two thousand years later, that simple, effective method of relaying information was still very much in use. In 1580, beacon fires were lit on almost every hill of the southern coast of England to warn the British of the approach of the Spanish Armada. And what about "One if by land, two if by sea?" A thrilling moment in American history—the North Church steeple lanterns that signaled Paul Revere to ride.

A Quantum Leap in Information Technology

In the last four hundred years, we have made a quantum leap in information technology. By the 1980s, if a Russian leader sneezes in Moscow, his ka-choo is transmitted instantly by satellite, the Soviet delegation to the United Nations can say "Gesundheit" in New York, and a few seconds later, they can hear "Thank you" back from the Kremlin.

Every day we are bombarded by an onslaught of information from the airwaves, from space, from our newspapers and magazines, by video clip and radiocast, and even by headlines spelled out in lights blinking around public buildings. At best, most of this bombardment is unnecessary overload. Much of the time, it's simply junk. At worst, however, it's dangerously misleading.

Let's face it—to many people junk food is delicious. The purveyors of junk food load it heavily with proven taste-bud provokers—sugar, salt, frying oils. They package it neatly in cute little containers and advertise it *ad nauseam*. But, tempting though it may appear, and appetizing as it may be manufactured to smell, it offers little in the way of nourishment. You can't live on junk food indefinitely or exclusively and remain healthy.

The healthy mind, the expanding mind, cannot thrive on junk food for the brain. It must become selective and *fast!* Because it's not getting any younger.

ALWAYS REMEMBER THAT THERE IS MORE
INFORMATION THAN TRUTH.

The Ascending Scale is simple, but it's helpful to keep it in mind as you're Brain Building. Picture it as a pyramid.

As you see, the Ascending Scale is a refining process, like panning for gold. First, you scoop up a panful of raw material from a promising riverbed. That's the Information which comes at us ceaselessly. Then you discard most of it as debris, selecting only those pieces which show signs of being likely to contain gold. They are the Data. Hidden in the Data are the facts, which do contain gold, but which must be put through a cleansing and refining process to remove impurities and reveal its perfections. Then, and only then, are you rewarded by the gleam of purest gold, the Truth.

Information is only the first step to Data, and Data only the next step to Fact. Fact is on the road to Truth, but it has a long way to go. And don't ever confuse Information with Truth, or you'll wind up with a panful of dirt, or at best, fool's gold.

Exercise: Envision investigating a new medical insurance policy. The companies will send you reams of information. From that, you will discard the glossy brochures with happy patients smiling from their sick beds, and you will keep the descriptions of the policies. That's the data. From the data, you will dig out the facts—what is covered and what is not. From the facts, you will be able to select the best policy in truth.

BRAIN BUILDER #111

CONSIDER THE SOURCE.

Know exactly who and what it is feeding you information before you swallow or digest it. Chew the information thoroughly first. We've talked before about how people unconsciously select slanted or biased newspapers, magazines, and other sources of information and "opinion" to buttress their own beliefs. By now you should be out of that habit. Nevertheless, such publications are often unavoidable in train stations, airports, and dentist's offices. They are packaged temptingly, with color spreads or with screaming sensational headlines. If you happen to pick one up, be aware of its bias as you turn the pages.

Exercise: From now on, choose your own information instead of letting others do it for you. Take your *own* magazine to the train station, the airport, and the dentist's office. But don't make the mistake of stopping at the newsstand on the way and buying one. That's just as bad as picking up one from the pile in your doctor's office. Instead, bring something from home—a magazine or book that you have already selected as being worthy enough to *spend* time with. Never just *kill* time by reading.

BRAIN BUILDER #112

LEARN TO DISTILL FACTS FROM COMMENTARY.

As a blatant example, take the description of an abortion clinic. "Family planning" or "baby slaughterhouse"? Although the latter statement is very obviously loaded, so in fact is the former. It's what is called a "euphemism," from the Greek idea of "speaking well" of something unpleasant (or terrifying or evil) so that it ceases to hold terror and presents a brighter face. Using that same euphemism, Hitler's massacre of millions could be termed "community planning"; in fact, Hitler had a euphemism of his own "the final solution"—as though the people destroyed were merely a problem to be solved. The point here is not whether abortions should be legal but that *both terms are descriptions intended to mold opinion.*

Probably the greatest difficulty in distilling facts from commentary is telling the difference. The words you hear spoken on the news have often been so homogenized that the milk of commentary and the cream of fact are blended so completely you can't tell where one leaves off and the other begins.

Understand that a lot of the time this isn't even done consciously. There's no conspiracy to defraud here, no threat to the national security. It's simply a matter of each person in power (and this includes those who write the news as well as those who make it) having his or her own political beliefs. This fact causes each speech or program to be slanted in that particular direction. Overt instructions to slant the news are quite unnecessary. Every employee knows that the fastest route to advancement is to please the boss and fit into the organization.

Many television news programs actually employ "commentators," media stars who are paid to deliver a one-sided opinion of national and world events. They tell you up front that this is their commentary and doesn't reflect anything but that. Presumably, the viewer is meant to believe that the rest of the news is therefore free of slant or bias. But to believe that is as naive as believing that newspapers run unbiased stories *off* the editorial pages and out of the purview of its columnists. That just doesn't happen.

If you find all this fairly harmless and believe that the conservative press and the liberal press will balance each other out, consider this. The media are not at all a cross-section of the people in this country. They do not represent the people at large any more than an organization of lawyers, plumbers, or secretaries represent all the people. They are nothing more than an occupational group, yet they possess far more power than a union of plumbers.

This exercise might make it easier for you to distill fact from commentary:

Exercise: If your tendencies are liberal, read conservative newspapers and listen to conservative newscasts. If you lean toward the conservative, do the reverse. This is not an exercise in tolerance, in "seeing the other side." Rather, it is an effort to help you notice the slanted, loaded language and the mechanism by which the "news" is personalized according to who delivers it to you.

But bear in mind that when you distill facts from commentary, you might wind up with nothing at all.

BRAIN BUILDER #113

CUT DOWN ON YOUR NEWSPAPER READING.

Read only the first few paragraphs of the substantive articles in the first few pages of your daily newspaper (not a tabloid, of course). This will give you a good ten-minute overview of the news worth knowing, nearly all of which is in the first few pages, and it will spare you the more partisan details which creep deeper and deeper into the story as it continues.

Exercise: For the next thirty days, read only the first three pages of your daily newspaper, but read them entirely, not only the articles which attract your attention. Reading only the first three pages will help you focus on the real reason you read the newspaper—for information, and not to kill time. (Reading *all* of them will help you learn about the subjects about which you know little, and which therefore interest you less. You shouldn't fool yourself into thinking that you're following the news when all you're following is the latest sensational jury trial.) For the following thirty days, cut back to reading only the first few paragraphs of every article in the first few pages. After that, read only what interests you, and I hope that "only" will be considerably broadened and deepened by that time.

VARY THE DAILY NEWSPAPER YOU READ.

If you buy a newspaper every day, buy a different one every day. If you subscribe to a newspaper, order one for weekdays and a different one for Sundays. Reading from more than one viewpoint not only increases the value of your information but also helps you gain an intellectual perspective.

Exercise: For the next six months, one month at a time, alternate a daily newspaper subscription between a leading liberal newspaper and a leading conservative newspaper. In other words, read the liberal point of view the first month, then the conservative point of view the next month, and so on.

GET LESS NEWS.

Get the news only once a day at the most. Unless there's an event of critical interest unfolding, absorbing the news once a day—from all media combined—is plenty. Once you've selectively read the first few pages of the daily paper, you'll have no need to listen to radio news or watch television news. And hearing the same thing several times a day comes perilously close to sounding like killing time.

Whenever someone says to me, "The only thing I watch on television is the news," I can only answer that I feel sorry for them, and that the news is one of the *worst* things to watch on television. Not only is it as partisan as it can be, it is also superficial and sensationalized.

Exercise: This week, get the news only once a day and only from the radio. Next week, get the news only once a day and only from the television. The following week, get the news only once a day and only from the newspaper. (At this point, it should be very clear why you should turn to the newspaper permanently.)

GET EVEN LESS NEWS THAN THAT.

Take a weekly one-day hiatus from the news. Let's take the case of the famous Sunday paper with its multiple sections. If you live in a large metropolis, this bible of journalism becomes heavier and heavier to carry as fall creeps toward Christmas, not because it contains more information or better information, but because of the radical increase in advertising. Advertisers are aware that there are hundreds of thousands of people in this country who seem to believe that Sunday exists only to yield up the Sunday paper.

Reading the Sunday paper is by no means a simple production. It usually calls for a cast of at least two people. One gets the life-style section and the book section, the other takes sports and the first section of the news. Both fight over the magazine and the theatrical section, and each sneaks a peek at the comics.

Then the couple retires to waste a perfectly good, useful, often beautiful day. As the sun's chariot rolls across the sky, they spend hours reading about plays they will never see, about books they will never buy or take from the library; he reads about athletic games that are already over, she about clothing she cannot afford sold in shops she has no time to visit. They read recipes for time-consuming dishes they will not cook, household hints they will not follow, and interviews with film stars who have little to say except that their latest motion pictures, coincidentally just being released to a theater near you, are the best work they've ever done. And all those precious hours slip away from them, time that can never be recalled.

If only I could wean you away from the Sunday newspaper and restore to you the gift of that time, it would justify the cost of this book. But I'm not fooling myself that you can go cold turkey on the Sunday paper, so why not give up another day for a start? Every week, try to go newsless for just one day. Believe it or not, the world will still be there when you get back.

Exercise: For the next month, don't read the newspaper on Wednesdays. For the following month, don't read the newspaper on Wednesdays and Saturdays. After sixty days, you can decide for yourself whether you've missed anything.

BRAIN BUILDER #117

READ MORE, BUT READ SELECTIVELY.

Exercise: Get a copy of the *New York Times* bestseller list, pick the one book that you think is the most worthwhile among the top twenty, and buy it to read.

The very act of reading is so important to your intellectual development that most reading will be of benefit. In fact, it's much easier to list what *not* to read. Don't waste your precious time on:

- Junk fiction. This is fiction at its worst, the concocted, hastily-written potboilers that often sell in the millions. These are not to be confused with intelligently-written modern novels or such good genre fiction as John le Carré's thrillers or P.D. James's murder mysteries. If you're reading to escape, however, why not escape into the world of Dickens? Or Dostoevsky? Or Wolfe? The plots are just as thrilling, and the characters far better-drawn and more true to life. If you truly can't spend the time meeting the demands placed on your thought processes by a great novel, a less challenging good one will have to do. Yet I wonder—if you're going to read 200 good pages, why not enrich the time with 200 great pages?

- Unauthorized modern biographies. This is nonfiction at its worst. If you want to read about a famous person, read the work of an author who isn't paid to sensationalize.

- Gossip magazines. These rank (and the word is appropriate) with the unauthorized biographies. If you *must* have a dose of this junk food now and then, scan them at the supermarket checkout line while you wait and put them back in the rack.

- Free political or religious magazines. Beware of these "giveaways"; they are intended to suborn your thinking and make converts to their philosophy. Anybody can proselytize, but these groups have made it an art form.

- Tabloid newspapers. These combine the worse aspects of the gossip rags and the instant bios and have the nerve to present it as news.

- Condensed novels. They are akin to food from which the vitamins and minerals have been extracted and thrown away. Worse, reading them makes you feel you've gained something when in fact you've lost something—more of your precious time. This is also true for those works abridged for children. The value of a good book is rarely in its story and never in its story alone. It's in the language, writing style, and the author's unique vision.

BRAIN BUILDER #118

DON'T READ FOR INFORMATION.

For one thing, the "information" may not be true or valid; it may be distorted. Pull back to an objective perspective when you read anything in nonfiction. In other words, read to achieve understanding. When you are enlightened by a book, you are neither convinced nor persuaded. *The concepts are not interchangeable.*

Exercise: Pick up the nearest magazine and look at a full-page ad. That's information.

The following quotation is from *How to Read A Book,* by Mortimer J. Adler and Charles Van Doren, published by Simon & Schuster; it's a book I recommend highly.

> The fourth and highest level of reading we will call Syntopical Reading. It is the most complex and systematic type of reading of all. . . . Another name for this level might be comparative reading. When reading syntopically, the reader reads many books, not just one, and places them in relation to one another and to a subject about which they all revolve. But mere comparison of texts is not enough. Syntopical reading involves more. With the help of the books read, the syntopical reader is able to construct an analysis of the subject that *may not be in any of the books.* . . . Let us suffice for the moment to say that syntopical reading is not an easy art, and that the rules for it are not widely known. Nevertheless, syntopical reading is probably the most rewarding of all reading activities. The benefits are so great that it is well worth the trouble of learning how to do it.

BRAIN BUILDER #119

DON'T DECIDE WHICH "SIDE" THE AUTHOR IS ON.

This is perhaps the most important thing to remember when reading nonfiction. Unless the book is only a few sentences long, you simply can't agree with everything the writer has to say, or disagree with it all. There are rarely only two sides to a question. Most issues are far more complex than that, involving many sides and many possible answers. Read for enlightenment.

Exercise: Stop telling people whether you "liked" or "didn't like" what you've read. That shouldn't be what's important! You like sugar, don't you? The point is whether you understood it.

In that vein, here are more quotes from Adler and Van Doren's *How to Read a Book*:

One of the most familiar tricks of the orator or propagandist is to leave certain things unsaid, things that are highly relevant to the argument, but that might be challenged if they were made explicit.

You must be able to say, with reasonable certainty, "I understand," before you can say any one of the following things: "I agree," or "I disagree," or "I suspend judgment." These three remarks exhaust all the critical positions you can take.

Do not agree or disagree. Always suspend judgment. It will, in the end, make you intellectually powerful.

BRAIN BUILDER #120

BUILD YOUR OWN REFERENCE LIBRARY.

When you're hungry, there's food in your refrigerator. If you're suddenly cold, there's a sweater hanging in your closet. But when your mind reaches out for a certain piece of information, is there a book in your home that will satisfy it?

Exercise: Go to the reference room of the best library you have locally and really look around, as if for the first time. If you've never been there before, or if you've only looked up what you needed at that moment and then left immediately, you're probably in the dark about just how much there is available to you.

Every time you feel the lack of an answer, write down the question. Very soon, a pattern representing your interests will emerge. You have already assembled a good basic first aid kit, so perhaps now is the time to specialize. Visit your library's reference department, and look at what's available. It will surprise you. Many good reference books are available as paperbacks; others may be purchased secondhand. Yard sales, church bazaars, and, especially, book fairs—often sponsored by the library or nonprofit community groups— are good places to find good books at low prices.

Buy as many as your budget allows; the finds are often fantastic, and there's no such thing as too many books. I'd rather look at a wall of books than a wall of paint, wouldn't you?

BRAIN BUILDER #121

WATCH TELEVISION SELECTIVELY.

Exercise: Each day for a week, write down every television show you watch and why. At the end of the week, look back at your list and take stock. Are you watching television only because you didn't feel like doing anything else? Is it an escape from reality? Are you better off now?

Television is another matter entirely from reading. With so many channels broadcasting for so many hours a day, so much of it mindless, situation comedies and situation trage-dies like potato chips for the brain, it becomes far easier to tell you what to *watch* than what to *avoid*.

If you're serious about Brain Building, these are programs that will not insult your intelligence:

- Great Performances (dance, music, drama)
- Larry King (interview)
- Late Night With David Letterman (comedy)
- Masterpiece Theater (drama)
- Monty Python's Flying Circus (comedy)
- Mystery! (detective drama)
- National Geographic Specials (science)
- Nova (science)
- nearly everything on public television

BRAIN BUILDER #122

USE ORIGINAL SOURCES.

Try not to get your information from secondary or "pass-along" sources. In order to avoid distortion, misinterpretation, or abridgment, keep returning to original sources. If somebody keeps talking about an article he's read in *Scientific American*, listen only for an understanding of a new perspective. Then go back and read the actual article for information. For comprehension, people are helpful, but for information, go to books.

Exercise: If you're going to write a report about Albert Schweitzer, quote Schweitzer himself. If you're going to give a talk about Darwin, quote Darwin himself.

BRAIN BUILDER #123

KEEP YOUR INTELLECTUAL BLOOD PRESSURE LOW.

You want to take a class, but you're afraid it's too hard for you to do well in, and that it might bring your grade point average down. Then audit the class instead, forgoing the grade and the credit. You won't have to take exams or turn in papers, but you will get a relaxed introduction to the information you're seeking.

You hesitate to attend a lecture on a topic about which you know nothing because the information is specialized. Go to the lecture, but forget about taking notes or trying to keep up. Just see if you can get a useful overview of the subject. If you can, it may be something to pursue on another occasion. And don't ever think of yourself as a dummy; dummies don't go to lectures.

Don't pass up reading books beyond your current understanding. These are the very books that are good for you. But if you're not ever going to read them, don't let them make you feel guilty by their very presence.

Exercise: Give away a few of the books sitting on your shelf, books that you feel you "should" read, but that you know you never will.

How much of what you've read has been of value to you? How much of what you've watched on television has been of value to you? How much of what you've heard on the radio has been of value to you?

Reading is the best way to stand on the intellectual shoulders of others. Just as you don't have to re-invent the light bulb to make use of it, you needn't re-create the works of the great thinkers to enjoy them and profit from them. George Orwell has already gone to the trouble of writing 1984. All you have to do is *read* it.

Perhaps the greatest value of "standing on another's shoulders" is this:

How do you know whether you should believe things for which you have no evidence? There's not enough time in your life for you to gather and sift through the evidence relating to everything you believe. No matter how intelligent or even intellectual you are, you will be forced to rely on others for some information. And there's the critical point of the matter: are you relying upon information, or are you relying on opinion?

191

You *should* believe the earth is round. The evidence is ample, including photographs taken from space. But even if you could personally examine every scrap of evidence, you haven't the expertise to interpret it. There aren't enough hours in a lifetime to become expert in everything.

But be aware that just because a belief is widespread does *not* mean it is true. Look at how many conflicting religions there are; can all of them be true? Obviously not. Moreover, there are many, many things that almost nobody disputes that are dead wrong. Galileo was arrested by the Inquisition for supporting the Copernican theory of astronomy that said the earth moved around the sun and the sun was the center of a solar system. In the 1600s, almost everybody believed that the earth, the home of Man, was the center of the universe. Almost everybody was wrong.

And maybe Einstein was wrong about time slowing down at high speeds, and maybe the astronauts of the future, returning from decades-long trips to the outward edges of our galaxy, will be just as old as the people they left behind.

When you begin to learn the difference between information and opinion, you are on your way to expanding your intellect.

Have You Thought as Much as You Thought You Have?

Ten subjects are listed below. How did you form your ideas about each of them? Among the sources listed beneath each, choose your major source of influence. And be honest with yourself.

1. MUSIC

A) RADIO	F) PERSONAL EXPERIENCE
B) TELEVISION	G) NEWSPAPERS
C) PULPIT	H) NEWS MAGAZINES
D) FAMILY	I) CLASSROOM
E) FRIENDS	J) BOOKS

2. ART

A) RADIO	F) PERSONAL EXPERIENCE
B) TELEVISION	G) NEWSPAPERS
C) PULPIT	H) NEWS MAGAZINES
D) FAMILY	I) CLASSROOM
E) FRIENDS	J) BOOKS

3. MORALITY

A) RADIO	F) PERSONAL EXPERIENCE
B) TELEVISION	G) NEWSPAPERS
C) PULPIT	H) NEWS MAGAZINES
D) FAMILY	I) CLASSROOM
E) FRIENDS	J) BOOKS

4. MARRIAGE

A) RADIO	F) PERSONAL EXPERIENCE
B) TELEVISION	G) NEWSPAPERS
C) PULPIT	H) NEWS MAGAZINES
D) FAMILY	I) CLASSROOM
E) FRIENDS	J) BOOKS

5. MINORITIES

A) RADIO	F) PERSONAL EXPERIENCE
B) TELEVISION	G) NEWSPAPERS
C) PULPIT	H) NEWS MAGAZINES
D) FAMILY	I) CLASSROOM
E) FRIENDS	J) BOOKS

6. SEX

A) RADIO	F) PERSONAL EXPERIENCE
B) TELEVISION	G) NEWSPAPERS
C) PULPIT	H) NEWS MAGAZINES
D) FAMILY	I) CLASSROOM
E) FRIENDS	J) BOOKS

7. SUCCESS

A) RADIO	F) PERSONAL EXPERIENCE
B) TELEVISION	G) NEWSPAPERS
C) PULPIT	H) NEWS MAGAZINES
D) FAMILY	I) CLASSROOM
E) FRIENDS	J) BOOKS

8. POLITICS

A) RADIO	F) PERSONAL EXPERIENCE
B) TELEVISION	G) NEWSPAPERS
C) PULPIT	H) NEWS MAGAZINES
D) FAMILY	I) CLASSROOM
E) FRIENDS	J) BOOKS

9. SCIENCE

A) RADIO	F) PERSONAL EXPERIENCE
B) TELEVISION	G) NEWSPAPERS
C) PULPIT	H) NEWS MAGAZINES
D) FAMILY	I) CLASSROOM
E) FRIENDS	J) BOOKS

10. RELIGION

A) RADIO	F) PERSONAL EXPERIENCE
B) TELEVISION	G) NEWSPAPERS
C) PULPIT	H) NEWS MAGAZINES
D) FAMILY	I) CLASSROOM
E) FRIENDS	J) BOOKS

Here is how to score this test. Give yourself points as follows:

Total number of A's _____ × 1 point = _____

Total number of B's _____ × 2 points = _____

Total number of C's _____ × 3 points = _____

Total number of D's _____ × 4 points = _____

Total number of E's _____ × 5 points = _____

Total number of F's _____ × 6 points = _____

Total number of G's _____ × 7 points = _____

Total number of H's _____ × 8 points = _____

Total number of I's _____ × 9 points = _____

Total number of J's _____ × 10 points = _____

Total number of points _____

The above ten sources are arranged according to the degree of detail and intellectual selectivity with which they offer you information. Spoken sources, for the most part, offer the least benefit unless they are combined with written sources, such as those found within a traditional or conventional classroom.

In addition to the total number you scored, count which category you checked most and look it up below. Next, regardless of your category high score, you should read all the score explanations below so that you may gain perspective on the various levels of scoring. After all, your thinking levels on the topics listed may have varied greatly from one to another.

Overall, however, a low score indicates an immaturity in the decision-making process. A high score indicates the reverse. Fifty is an average score, but it's no compliment, and you'll see why.

Score by Categories

Category	# of Points
A) RADIO	1–10

Worse than poor. If you scored only in this range, you have never received information from any source other than the radio in your life, and, so far as the normal intellect is concerned, you couldn't be in worse shape. Radio is almost entirely entertainment and offers you virtually no information other than the news.

B) TELEVISION   11–20

Poor. For the most part, you haven't risen above the radio and television level. While television offers more information than radio does, particularly on the public channels, it's still nearly all entertainment. Programs such as Carl Sagan's *Cosmos* series and Dr. Richard Restak's *The Brain* series are rare, unfortunately.

C) PULPIT   21–30

Better than poor. If you're at the pulpit level, at least you're beginning to listen to live people rather than disembodied voices over the radio and television. Keep in mind, however, that religion classes and religious books belong in the "pulpit" category and not in the "classroom" or "books" category.

D) FAMILY   31–40

Worse than fair. Of the word-of-mouth variety of intellectual growth, your family isn't bad, and your parents are probably the best among that group. Unfortunately, it is very difficult for them to relate to you as an equal, so information will be "told" to you, rather than shared with you, putting you at the mercy of whoever by genetic chance happens to be raising you.

E) FRIENDS   41–50

Fair. Although this is certainly moving up, your friends and acquaintances are unlikely to know much more than you do, rendering them incapable of helping you very much. Also, if they're people you see for their entertaining side, rather than their serious side, they won't even bother to try, unless you've chosen your friends wisely. Unlike family however, at least with friends, you get to *choose*.

F) PERSONAL EXPERIENCE   51–60

Better than fair. At least you've begun to find things out for yourself. Of course, you'll never get far if you don't move across to the written word, but experiencing things for yourself is at least better for building your intellect than simply reprocessing received information.

G) NEWSPAPERS   61–70

Almost good. Now you're getting closer to the broad kind of information you need for perspective and intellectual growth. Certain newspapers, *The New York Times*, for example, are far above this level, ranking more like the classroom and, in some cases, even the book level.

H) NEWS MAGAZINES   71–80

Good. News magazines are able to go into depth on the more important subjects the way newspapers can't. Newspapers are obligated to report "all" the news, but news magazines are free to focus on the news that requires more thought. Fortunately, there are some extremely good ones.

I) CLASSROOM   81–90

Very good. At this level, you are undoubtedly getting information from the top four levels and can flex a good bit more intellectual muscle than the average person. Classroom education is difficult to top for gaining perspective. Unfortunately, most people simply repeat what their professors taught them, and they are not even aware that, if they'd had different professors, they'd be repeating something else.

J) BOOKS   91–100

Excellent. It's hard to top classroom education, but in the intellectual arena, books are the winner. Most of the classroom education you get will be specialized. And if your education is too broad, you might not even be able to get a job with your degree. Either way, you'll develop more intellectual power each time you read a book in the humanities, in school or out of it.

Looking back over this quiz as a whole, you'd do well to keep two things in mind. If you had an average score, remember that there's nothing wrong with getting all your ideas from your parents initially, but that they should be only early, initial sources, not major ones or primary ones. If your parents are still your major source of information, you are either very young or you haven't completed your self-analysis yet. You may not even have begun it.

Use What You Read

On the other hand, reading a great many books can certainly help you become informed, but if you can do no more than repeat what you've read, you haven't built your brain or accomplished anything useful with your intellect. You must use what you read. Even fiction—if it's good—is useful as insight into the human heart and the human condition.

HERE'S THE QUIZ FOR WEEK NINE

1) With the computer metaphor for the mind, what is the hardware and what is the software?
2) Is all information roughly equal?
3) What is a "euphemism"?
4) Which is the best paragraph of a newspaper article to read?
5) What's the worst thing to watch on television?
6) Which is the worst newspaper to read?
7) What book did I recommend?
8) Does it make sense to attend classes without receiving credit?
9) How do we know Einstein was right?
10) What element is the key to becoming an intellectual?

ANSWERS

1) Intellect is the hardware; information is the software.
2) No! Much of it is just junk.
3) It's an inoffensive expression for something offensive.
4) The first one. It has the most information.
5) The advertising.
6) The Sunday paper. It wastes the most time.
7) *How to Read a Book*, by Mortimer Adler and Charles Van Doren.
8) Yes! Credit isn't the point; learning is.
9) We don't. He may have been wrong.
10) Learning the difference between information and opinion.

CHAPTER

13

WEEK TEN

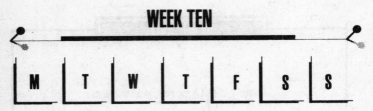

| M | T | W | T | F | S | S |

Building Comprehension

TOOLS YOU WILL NEED FOR WEEK TEN:
A good mystery novel and a nonfiction book you enjoy.

Nature that framed us of our elements . . . doth teach us all
to have aspiring minds: Our souls, whose faculties can comprehend to wondrous Architecture of the world . . .

—Christopher Marlowe

The act of comprehension means, quite literally, to take
hold of something mentally, to grasp it, much in the way
that the New World monkey grasps a swinging vine with
his prehensile tail. In comprehension, the idea itself is
more important than the sum of its parts; it's the *totality*
you're going for, and the details can be sketched in later.

The Light Bulb: Turn It On in Your Mind

Take a simple example—a common household light bulb. It's possible to comprehend how electricity works without going into a study of stationary or moving charges and elementary particles. It is observable in nature—in lightning, in electric eels. We know it is carried across the nation inside huge power lines. We are aware that the light switch we hit on our wall either releases the current or arrests its flow to the bulb's filament. When the current is released, the bulb lights up; when it's arrested, the bulb goes dark. If the filament burns out or breaks, we throw the bulb away and screw in another one. Even without a master's degree in physics, we comprehend enough about the light bulb so that we don't have to re-invent it every time we use it.

This is the simplest form of comprehension, and it has its day-to-day uses. To know more we would have to learn more, but there are only twenty-four hours in anyone's day. Comprehension is the big, overall picture that the intelligent mind *grasps*, and Brain Building will help you strengthen that grasp so that you will comprehend better, faster, and more completely.

BRAIN BUILDER #124

STUDY WHAT YOU ENJOY.

Exercise: Telephone your local community college and ask for a list of adult education courses. At least read the list all the way through.

Comprehension comes far more easily when tension is not present, and you'll feel far more relaxed when dealing with a subject you genuinely enjoy, even if it's not a particularly important one. And you'll do better with something to which you have a natural attraction or for which you have some talent or ability. Don't feel guilty about doing what you like; that's what everybody wants, deep down: to work at something they like.

In the same way, unless it's assigned for class, don't pick up a boring book, no matter how "good for you" it is or how much you feel obliged to read it. It will stifle your comprehension, not expand it. There are plenty of great things to read that will excite you and be worth every minute of your precious time. This is not to say that you shouldn't take up a *challenging* book, one beyond your present comprehension. To confuse boring with difficult is to rob yourself of potential for expanding your intelligence. Just because you don't fully understand a certain complex concept *now* doesn't mean you *can't* understand it or *will* never understand it. A challenge is the very opposite of boring. The very word "challenge" should stand for "stimulating" or "exciting." The next Brain Builder will show you a good way to read beyond your present comprehension.

BRAIN BUILDER #125

READ FROM BEGINNING TO END.

Exercise: When reading nonfiction for retention, don't slow down, and don't stop to figure out what you don't understand. Instead of stopping to puzzle out what appears incomprehensible at first, read the book straight through to the end at the same rate at which you would read an enjoyable piece of fiction. Then go back and read it again. You'll find that, now that you have the overall picture, much of what eluded you the first time around will all fit into place. Also, any sort of repetition strengthens retention. Compare this with seeing a baffling mystery film twice. The second time around, when you know what's going to happen, the individual scenes are much clearer to you.

Exercise: Go to any good university bookstore and scan the shelves for the simplest text that deals with any subject you like a lot. Now, here's the key to success for this exercise: don't allow yourself to be diverted to a subject you've always thought you *should* know something about. Instead, pick a subject you've always loved. If the book is a little *too* simple, look for a slightly more difficult text until you find one that contains some things you don't already know about the subject. Then, take it home and—at your leisure—enjoy reading about something you like, thereby furthering your education at the same time, and never going back to reread anything, whether on the same page or in the same chapter. Just have a leisurely read-through of the entire book, from beginning to end, at a comfortable pace.

Then, if you wish, *and only if you wish*, go back and read it a second time. This is an excellent way to take the pressure off learning and allow it to be the delight it used to be before you had education forced upon you. When you finish that book, whether in the first week of reading or two months later, repeat the exercise with a different text on the same subject.

READ THE LAST CHAPTER OF A MYSTERY FIRST.

This is the converse-yet-corollary of the above exercise, but using fiction.

Exercise: Get hold of a good paperback detective novel, one with real clues instead of violence (such as an Agatha Christie Hercule Poirot or Miss Marple), and read the last chapter first. Then go back to page one and read it through. You won't enjoy much suspense, but this isn't an exercise in suspense. Rather, it's an exercise in learning *how* to comprehend. Once you know what the outcome will be, you can pay attention to all the little cues and clues sprinkled liberally throughout. Bits and pieces of the puzzle, which you might easily miss if you didn't know the ending, will fall into place.

LISTEN TO THE UNFAMILIAR WITHOUT CRITICISM.

Again, you are after the big picture here, the total comprehension of the work, whatever it is, so don't argue. Instead, try to get as much out of it as you can, and in the most positive way.

Besides, anyone can tear something down. Being able to build it in the first place is what counts. Whom do you admire more, the person who builds a home or the person who sets a match to it? If you have developed the habit of building yourself up by tearing others down, this is the perfect time to stop, now, when you're building comprehension by absorbing without criticism.

The first thing to do is to consciously withhold all the critical words which unconsciously rise to your lips. Make this a habit.

Exercise: If you're a Republican, attend a Democratic rally or meeting. If you're a Democrat, attend a Republican rally or meeting. In both cases, keep your ears and your mind open *and your mouth shut!*

The next thing is to "compete" in the area you are criticizing.

Exercise: Turn your own hand to the same kind of work or thought you have criticized. You'll be surprised at how rapidly your desire to find fault will abate when you learn firsthand the problems involved in the job.

BRAIN BUILDER #128

SIT IN THE FRONT.

Always position yourself as closely as possible to your learning device. Sit at the front of any meeting you attend or class you are taking—not to impress your instructor (the class may be so large, he or she will never learn your name)—but to absorb more without the visual and audio distraction you encounter when there are people between you and your source of information.

Exercise: The next time you take a guided tour around an art gallery or monument, try trailing at the outer edge of the group for the first half of the tour, then walking next to the guide for the second half. You'll see the difference.

BRAIN BUILDER #129

CONCENTRATE ON THE SUBJECT.

When you listen to educational cassettes, close your eyes and use a headset instead of earphones. Covering both ears limits the distracting sensory input and allows you to concentrate better. Likewise, when watching educational video cassettes, darken the room and close it off to outside noise.

Exercise: Take out an audiocassette and listen to it while walking around the house. Then sit down and listen to it with your eyes closed. Hear the difference?

BRAIN BUILDER #130

USE A MULTISENSORY APPROACH TO LEARNING.

If you find a subject difficult, or if you want to learn it especially well, use a multisensory approach wherever possible, even if you have to invent it. Bring as many of your senses to bear on the problem as you can. *Read* the words—as in a book—at the same time that you *listen* to the words—as with an audio cassette—and *"watch"* the words—as with an instructor. The more of your senses you use, the easier it will be to both comprehend and remember. *Speaking* the words out loud provides an additional useful dimension, and, in the case of youngsters in particular, *touching* is also of great help; it is useful to adults as well as children. Reading the manual for your new word-processing program is nothing compared to putting your fingers on the keys and tapping out the commands—a literal "hands-on" approach.

BRAIN BUILDER #131

DON'T THINK IN WORDS.

Thinking in words slows you down and actually decreases comprehension in much the same way as walking a tightrope too slowly makes one lose one's balance. Even *reading* in words rather than in the mental image they evoke will slow down your comprehension and your absorption of the material. Try to think in visual images larger than the words you're reading—try to envision the whole picture of the topic and where this particular section fits into that picture.

I find that "not thinking in words" increases intuitiveness because thinking in words narrows your reasoning to the concepts that you notice and for which you have words. When you pay overall attention to the situation without limiting your analysis to whatever few threads you can put into words, you will grasp more—although you may not know why. And this is what most people call intuition—although *they* don't know why!

Exercise: Read through the text following the next Brain Builder *extremely* slowly, word by word. Does it make more sense or less? That's what I mean.

BRAIN BUILDER #132

USE INTELLECTUAL SHORTHAND.

There are times when complex issues can be reduced to manageable size by making two lists: the positives and the negatives. When you've listed them, assign a number value— signifying its importance—to every item on the list, ranging from 1 to 100 for the positives and −1 to −100 for the negatives. Add up the columns, and you'll see immediately the general direction of the issue, while the numbers themselves will clarify how you feel about each item. The number of positives and negatives alone is less significant than the sum of their values.

Exercise: Before you come to a complex issue, practice a little intellectual shorthand now. Take a piece of lined paper and divide it in half lengthwise, then write at the top of each half the name of a friend about whom you feel ambivalent. Label one half "positive" and one half "negative." Do the positive half first, so that you won't feel guilty about writing down negatives and thus be tempted to list positives to compensate. (And don't go back and add to the positive half afterward, either.) List all the positive aspects of this person that you can think of in ten minutes. Then list the negative ones in the same way. When you've finished, assign a number value to each of the positive aspects. Then do the same to each of his or her negative qualities. Add them up. How does your friend fare overall? Positive or negative? Now do it again with a relative.

BRAIN BUILDER #133

DON'T TRUST YOUR FEELINGS.

Keep in mind that things aren't necessarily correct because they *feel* correct. Until the end of the sixteenth century, the world believed the Aristotelian theory that two objects of unequal weight (say, a marble and an apple) would fall at unequal speeds. It made perfect sense; it "felt" right. Who could expect a marble to plummet at the same rate as an apple? But around 1590, Galileo Galilei, in his experiments with falling bodies, proved that two different weights, released at the same moment, always *did* fall at the same rate of speed. What felt correct to so many for so many centuries was, in fact, wrong. It might have made sense, but it didn't make fact.

Exercise: Suppose you have a completely sealed truck carrying crates of birds. Will the truck weigh the same if the birds are in flight? The impulse to say "no" is common to many people—if the birds are up in the air, they don't weigh anything, do they? But science says "yes," the weight of the truck will not change. Here's why. The flying bird's body is supported by the air on which it glides just as the sitting bird's body is supported by the crate, and the air is sealed inside the truck. The entire weight is supported by the system sealed within that truck, and as long as none of the system can leak out, the truck will weigh the same. In other words, the bird weighs the same whether he's in flight or not.

The point here is not weight or birds or physics, but the fact that, when facts are in question, it is necessary to comprehension to follow the mind and not the heart. What may sound like the logical answer to a question of fact may (in fact) be dead wrong.

BRAIN BUILDER #134

UNDERSTAND BY EXPLAINING.

In order to comprehend something better, try explaining it to somebody else. Make certain it's something that you already understand well, but you'll find that formulating an explanation of the subject for someone else's comprehension will make you comprehend your subject even better. Skip no logical steps in your explanation. Once you are forced to put your comprehension to work, and in proper order, any gaps in it will be obvious, both to you and to your listener. In fact, his questions will be signpoints to increasing your understanding!

Exercise: You think you understand basic mathematics? Try explaining multiplication to a child.

Asking Questions Is a Powerful Tool

Now we come to one of the most important factors in the building of comprehension—the asking of questions. Believe it or not, this is in itself an art as well as a powerful tool used to increase your understanding and expand your intellect.

BRAIN BUILDER #135

ASK HONEST QUESTIONS.

Ask questions that are honestly designed to increase your comprehension instead of questions designed—even subconsciously—to impress the speaker or others. Asking showoff questions to persuade others that you are bright is a tactic easily seen through and one which will help your understanding not one whit.

Further, phrase your questions honestly and without challenge. If you can't understand what the speaker is driving at, don't ask "What do you mean by that?" There's a certain challenge in the question and even an implied insult. It's better to say, "In other words, do you feel . . . ?" If you're wrong, and you may well be wrong, the speaker will be quick to correct you without ill feeling.

Exercise: Rephrase the following annoying questions:
Why in the world would you do that?
Don't you know that won't work?
Is that really what you think?
Who told you that?

BRAIN BUILDER #136

QUESTION FOR INFORMATION.

Never ask questions in order to expose flaws in another's arguments. In our culture, asking questions is frequently perceived negatively, and for very good reasons. Questioning is often an effort to tear down, an effort that, by the way, usually proves fruitless. People simply won't allow their beliefs, correct or incorrect, to be torn apart by others. Why this should be so if the beliefs are incorrect is a matter apart. But understand that you will have little success in exposing others' mistaken beliefs by questioning them. Likewise, and much more importantly, others will have little success tearing yours apart; in this latter scenario, you are very much the loser. Before others question your longheld beliefs, question them yourself.

The only fruitful role of the questioner is a constructive one. Rather than tear down another's beliefs with your questions, therefore, learn to build your own on a foundation of logic and reason, through continual self-questioning.

Exercise: Listen to the questions at a presidential press conference to see which of them are asked for information and which are asked in order to convey a critical message to the listening audience or readership.

DON'T "QUESTION" PEOPLE.

Simply ask them questions. Almost nobody likes to be "questioned." ("Who are you?" "What do you want?") It feels inquisitional and invasive. Something else entirely is "asking questions." ("May I ask who's calling?" "May I help you?") The less personal your questions, the better. Phrase them as impersonally as possible.

Actually, you can learn a great deal from *both*—people who don't like to be questioned and people who do. The latter will impart knowledge about their ideas, the former, about human nature.

Exercise: The next time someone asks you a question that you find irritating, write it down afterward. Then, when you've cooled off, take a look at it and ask yourself whether you ask that question of *others*.

Here are some *other* reasons that people *don't* like to be questioned:

1) They're afraid they haven't been truthful with you.

2) They're afraid they haven't been truthful with themselves.

3) Like Father William in the Lewis Carroll poem, "You Are Old, Father William," they simply don't want to be bothered—"I have answered three questions and that is enough . . . Be off, or I'll kick you downstairs."

Here are some of the reasons that people *do* like to be questioned:

1) They're confident they're telling you the truth.

2) They're not afraid to uncover their weaknesses; actually, they welcome the opportunity to correct any errors in their thinking.

3) They may be in the business of imparting information, such as teachers.

ASK QUESTIONS OF THE RIGHT PERSON.

Do you ever, for example, ask advice of a person who is not an authority on the subject or successful in the area questioned? Let's say you're going to your mother for some personal advice. Ask yourself this question first: Is she an expert in the subject? Or have you constantly challenged her authority and expertise in personal matters? Are emotions involved or only reason? Questions should always be based on a genuine desire for comprehension; if you seek advice, find someone who's knowledgeable; then ask questions.

Exercise: Write down six practical questions that are on your mind right now. Then think about the best person you can reasonably ask about each one and write that down, too. Now look back at the list. Is that the person you're going to ask?

BREAK DOWN THE BARRIERS BETWEEN YOU AND
RATIONAL UNDERSTANDING.

Exercise: Make a brief list of everything that is wrong with automobiles, then look back at the list. Even the *best* things are easy to criticize, aren't they?

The Barriers to Comprehension

In any serious attempt to expand comprehension, attention must be paid to the barriers that stand between your intellect and true understanding. These barriers are the enemy of the independent brain; sad to say, they are not only common, they are rampant!

The first such enemy is emotion. Emotions color our thinking and impinge upon our intellect. Even so, many people regard it as a strength and are proud to be irrational; they cling to their emotion-tinged beliefs, claiming that it makes them "human" or "humanistic." As though the greatest rational philosophers in history weren't also humanists! Irrationality doesn't make anybody a better person.

The next barrier is the prior point of view, often carved in stone. If you yourself have one, you will unconsciously select material that reinforces it—news, editorials, books, stories, and so on. Or you will absorb such material in a way that reinforces it. There is no sound quite so doleful as the door to a mind clanging shut.

Even in the scientific arena, where one might expect reason to rule, there is often a problem. Scientists tend to process information according to *prior* information, although they are aware of that flaw and continually struggle against it. If this is such a problem for *them*, imagine how great a problem it is for the average person who is little inclined to self-examination or introspection!

Those who are not independent thinkers begin to see things selectively, to reinforce their previously-held beliefs. The process begins early in life, and the longer it's allowed to continue, the harder it will be to shake those erroneous beliefs. As with any habit, the longer you hold onto a misconception, the harder it is to let it go. That's one reason older people are often thought of as slow learners; they have a lot more unlearning to do. One of the reasons that children are able to learn so quickly is that their personalities aren't yet fully developed and planted firmly in front of their intellects. If you stay young intellectually, you'll learn better. Mental old age is often not so much a matter of hardening of the arteries as it is hardening of the attitudes.

The tendency toward justification of one's beliefs in the face of any challenge is also a barrier to increased comprehension. Everything, even ideas, can have bad aspects as well as good. Accept this, and don't try to pretend otherwise. It will weaken your position and not only make you look less intelligent, it will make you be less intelligent.

Your other ideas will also be suspect. A cat eating a canary is good only for the cat; for the canary, it's a catastrophe.

Some people feel the need to justify everything in nature, and some of them even carry it to extremes. The worst example of this that I've ever heard in person was a young woman who stated firmly that cancer was good because it helped hold down the human population! Let's examine this extraordinary justification of cancer: Is "holding down the human population" an innate good? If so, should we then allow the hunting of people in areas that are overcrowded? We could issue licenses—"permit to take one male, two females, three children." If cancer is good, can heart attacks be bad? Let's all increase our intake of salt, fatty meat, and rich desserts. Let's exercise less and light up another cigarette. If that doesn't work, how about bubonic plague? That did the job of population control in the Middle Ages. No, here is a definitive question to ask in the face of the young woman's absurd justification: If we didn't already have cancer in the world, would we choose it?

Another common thinking error is generalizing from personal experience. Let somebody take a certain medication for a kidney infection, and it's amazing how he'll push it on you for your own. A generalization from one's limited personal experience is even harder to dislodge than an ordinary hasty generalization. Worse, it narrows perspective, and only a broader perspective can help lead to a greater intelligence.

And the Greatest Barrier of All

But possibly the greatest barrier between anybody and a better intellect is the inability to admit mistakes. Crippled by this inability, how can the mind make brave strides forward?

It's somehow frightening to admit you're wrong. You wonder "If I'm wrong about this one important thing, what about everything else I believe?" The earth wobbles under your feet, causing anxiety and insecurity. But take heart. And take courage. The earth always wobbles when you're searching for the truth. Just understand this, and you won't expect the impossible or even the improbable. You'll understand how hard it is to own up to a mistake and go on from there, and you won't expect others to do it easily. But work on it for yourself. You can help your mental growth immeasurably by admitting it when you're wrong.

The problem worsens with age. If you've lived by and acted upon erroneous beliefs for many years, the thought of all that time wasted in error is positively intolerable. Someone who has devoted only three months to an error is far more likely to cast it aside than someone who has believed in it for three decades.

Here's a common error in thinking: *making a judgment based on a certain set of circumstances and clinging to that judgment after the circumstances have changed.* If the brain is to remain flexible, the mind open, then circumstances have to support judgments and must always be reviewed and re-evaluated.

A simple example of that: In Grandma's youth, short skirts, dark lipstick and nail polish, and untidy hair were never worn by "nice" girls, only by "fast" ones. Her grandson brings his girlfriend to meet her, and she is dressed in the height of teenage fashion—wearing a short denim skirt, high-heeled boots, many bracelets, and the rest of the New Wave look. Grandma's judgment is instantly negative—this cannot be a nice girl. She can't admit that circumstances have changed, that the younger woman's fashion look is in fact the 1990s equivalent of the long plaid skirt, scuffed saddle shoes, and oversize, button-up-the back sweater that Grandma herself wore as a teenager in the 1940s.

Another common error: *by proving someone else wrong, you prove yourself right, and "smarter."* What a pitfall, and how easy to tumble into it! It's easy to doubt everything. Some people who like to think of themselves as intellectuals make a hobby of doubting everything in and out of sight. But that's not good enough.

Take our old friend, the light bulb, again. It is riddled with flaws. It won't light up the world; it won't even light up your entire home or apartment. So what? So it has limitations? We knew that. So it'll break if you drop it? We knew that, too. We have accepted those limitations and can get around them. We use more than one bulb; we stock extra bulbs to replace the broken ones.

The so-called intellectual pretender will remain silent in darkness, but will curse the light bulb as soon as somebody else invents it, pointing out all its flaws.

The ineffectuals curse the darkness.

The effectuals create the light bulbs.

The psuedo-intellectuals curse the light bulb.

The effective intellectual tells us objectively things about the light bulb we never knew before—both unknown strengths and weaknesses.

Brief Quiz

A QUIZ FOR THE END OF WEEK TEN

1) What does "comprehension" have to do with a monkey's tail?
2) What should you do if you don't understand what you're reading?
3) Where's the best place to sit in the classroom?
4) What's the best approach to learning?
5) Should you think in words?
6) Can you trust common sense?
7) When should you try explaining something to someone else?
8) Can everything be justified in some way?
9) What was your favorite subject in school?
10) Have you ever studied it since you left school?

ANSWERS

1) "Comprehension" and "prehensile tails" both grasp things.
2) Continue to read the entire text. Then read it again.
3) Right in front of the instructor.
4) A multisensory approach.
5) No. It slows you down.
6) No.
7) Only when you know the subject well. Then the experience will be good for both of you.
8) No. (For example, I can find nothing good in the wearing of high heels.)
9) And if you said "girls" or "lunch," try this question again.
10) If not, I strongly suggest that you go out and find a course in the subject and sign up for it as soon as possible. If that's impossible, at least go out and treat yourself to a book.

CHAPTER

14

WEEK ELEVEN

| M | T | W | T | F | S | S |

Building Perspective

TOOLS YOU WILL NEED FOR WEEK ELEVEN:
A full-sized, nonmagnifying hand-held mirror.

"Let observation with extensive view
Survey mankind from China to Peru."

—Dr. Samuel Johnson

Perspective is what gives you a vantage point on the world
as it is, not as you or others hope it will be. It is very closely
tied in with objectivity. If you view it from a mathematical

perspective, perspective itself is actually a subset of objectivity. Its value in expanding intelligence is immeasurable. A strong sense of perspective allows you to mentally step back, step forward, or to one side to view the circumstances and assess the facts. Only a realistic perspective or set of perspectives will give your intellect the tools it needs to form correct judgments, large and small. The development of objectivity is paramount in Brain Building, second only to the development of independent thinking.

BRAIN BUILDER #140

IMPROVE YOUR PERSPECTIVE.

Exercise: If you were a direct descendant of Julius Caesar, how many other descendants come between you and him? Quickly now, don't stop to think about it; don't figure it out with pencil and paper; just venture a guess. How many great-great-grandmothers would there be between now and those far-off days of antiquity?

Did you say hundreds? Most people do. Or did you say 61 grownups and a teenager, which is the actual number of "greats"? If you got that number, or anything near it, good for you; you already possess an admirable historical perspective.

Now let's figure it out. Julius Caesar went to his death in 44 B.C. which, as we figure dates, is a minus quantity. Add 44 B.C. to 1990 A.D., and the number of years between them is 2,034. But people are numbered by generations—defined as the time between the birth of a mother and the birth of her child, which obviously varies greatly from culture to culture. Our western culture commonly accepts three generations per century, or 33⅓ years per generation. Now divide 2,034 by 33⅓, and you'll find that only 61 generations stand between you and the last republican leader of ancient Rome.

Likewise, if William Shakespeare were your ancestor, only 11 (or so) generational descendants followed between the Bard of Avon, who died in 1616, and you today. You could probably fit that number into a buffet supper at your place.

Perception and Perspective

Stop and consider your perception of history and its perspective. "Antiquity," which seems lost in the mist of millennia, actually wasn't so long ago—only 61 33-year-olds stand between you and it. In the true perspective of human experience, Julius Caesar lived, loved, fought, and died only yesterday. Or take your individual perspective. Let's say you have a memory spanning fifty years. Only 41 such spans stretch between you and the death of Caesar.

Perspective is how we perceive the correct relationships and interrelationships of everything—time, space, events. Perspective is the most important ingredient in forming judgments about anything, from the conflict in the Middle East to whether your daughter (or son) should have her (or his) ears pierced. To build your perspective, you must first understand where you fit, and second, where those who came before you fit in the time line of history.

Possibly no subject is more underrated than history; too bad, because an understanding of history is one of the most important tools in basic intellectual functioning. History, as the Romans called it, is res gestae, the "doings of people." Which, of course, encompasses everything—the building of the pyramids, the flight out of Egypt, Archimedes' discovery of the principle of the lever, the rise of Islam, the discovery of gunpowder by the Chinese, Shakespeare's writing Twelfth Night, Mozart composing his incomparable music, the principle of the steam engine, Mme. Curie's discovery of radium, Neil Armstrong's giant step for mankind. Everything of note that men and women do immediately becomes history. Art, architecture, medicine, music, science, technology, literature, geography, mathematics—all are a part of the flow of human history.

BRAIN BUILDER #141

LOOK BACK IN TIME.

Learn the overview of history. Study a time line until you are familiar with the chronology of events. The first thing that you should recognize about the time line is that *it is unbroken*. Although we learn about "centuries" and "eras" and "ages" and "epochs" in the classroom, there is no such distinct separation in real time. Days follow one after another, adding up to weeks and months in an unbroken chain adding up to centuries followed by millennia. Everything that has happened so far in the history of humankind follows everything that happened before.

Exercise: On the next two pages are a basic time line of history, beginning with the earliest civilizations and ending with the present time. Study the time line until you have the chronology of events well in hand. The specific dates are not important, but the sequence of events is. In this exercise, understanding the events is less important than paying witness to the chronology. Don't memorize; don't agonize. Just read it a few times.

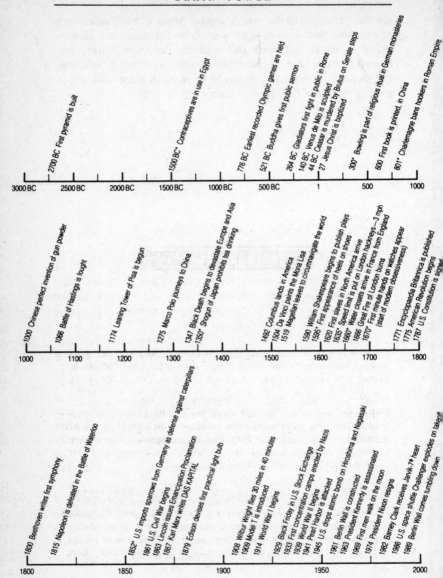

Timeline 1 — 3000 BC to 1000:
- 2700 BC First pyramid is built
- 1500 BC* Contraceptives are in use in Egypt
- 776 BC Earliest recorded Olympic games are held
- 521 BC Buddha gives first public sermon
- 264 BC Gladiators first fight in public in Rome
- 140 BC Venus de Milo is sculpted
- 44 BC Caesar is murdered by Brutus on Senate steps
- 27 Jesus Christ is baptized
- 300* Bowling is part of religious ritual in German monasteries
- 600 First book is printed, in China
- 801* Charlemagne bans hookers in Roman Empire

Timeline 2 — 1000 to 1800:
- 1000 Chinese perfect invention of gun powder
- 1066 Battle of Hastings is fought
- 1174 Leaning Tower of Pisa is begun
- 1275 Marco Polo journeys to China
- 1347 Black Death begins to devastate Europe and Asia
- 1350* Shogun of Japan prohibits tea drinking
- 1492 Columbus lands in America
- 1504 Da Vinci paints the Mona Lisa
- 1519 Magellan leaves to circumnavigate the world
- 1590 William Shakespeare begins to publish plays
- 1595* First appearance of heels on shoes
- 1620 First slaves in North America arrive
- 1635* Speed limit is put on London hackneys—3 mph
- 1660* Water closets arrive in France from England
- 1666 Great Fire of London burns
- 1670* First minute hands on watches appear (start of modern obsessiveness)
- 1771 Encyclopaedia Britannica is published
- 1775 American Revolution is begun
- 1787 U.S. Constitution is signed

Timeline 3 — 1800 to 2000:
- 1800 Beethoven writes first symphony
- 1815 Napoleon is defeated in the Battle of Waterloo
- 1852* U.S. imports sparrows from Germany as defense against caterpillars
- 1861 U.S. Civil War begins
- 1863 Lincoln issues Emancipation Proclamation
- 1867 Karl Marx writes DAS KAPITAL
- 1879 Edison devises first practical light bulb
- 1908 Wilbur Wright flies 30 miles in 40 minutes
- 1909 Model T is introduced
- 1914 World War I begins
- 1929 Black Friday in U.S. Stock Exchange
- 1933 First concentration camps erected by Nazis
- 1939 World War II begins
- 1941 Pearl Harbor is attacked
- 1945 U.S. drops atomic bomb on Hiroshima and Nagasaki
- 1961 Berlin Wall is constructed
- 1963 President Kennedy is assassinated
- 1969 First men walk on the moon
- 1974 President Nixon resigns
- 1982 Barney Clark receives Jarvik-7® heart
- 1986 U.S. space shuttle Challenger explodes on takeoff
- 1989 Berlin Wall comes tumbling down

The events marked with an asterisk are, well, a little less important.

Sources: CHRONOLOGY OF WORLD HISTORY by Freeman–Grenville

THE TIMETABLES OF HISTORY by Bernard Grun   ENCYCLOPAEDIA BRITANNICA

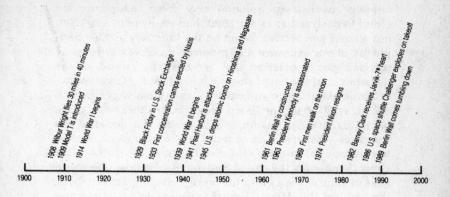

A Perspective on History

Imagine this: It's two o'clock on a Tuesday afternoon in Florence, Italy. The month is April, the year is 1300. A cloud darkens the sun briefly and, when it passes, the Middle Ages are over and everybody is now enjoying the Renaissance. Absurd? Of course it is. It's entirely the wrong perspective.

In the centuries after the spread of Christianity, many Europeans believed that history would come to an abrupt halt in the year 1000, that Christ would return at the millennium to judge the world, and everything would come to an end. As you can well imagine, there was some serious panic in Christian Europe during the late 900s. Everybody was expecting to die and be judged. Yet, one second after midnight on January 1, 1000, those same people were pinching themselves to make certain they were still alive. The millennium had come and gone, and it was just another day in the history of the world.

As we head into the 1990s, we are expecting the second millenium within the next five minutes, historically speaking. But in the intervening thousand years, humankind's perspective has changed, and most of us aren't running around putting our affairs in order and trying to find a sitter for the cat.

The Church is no longer the powerful ruling body it was in the year A.D. 999. Eternity does not threaten modern man,

219

although nuclear annihilation may. Even though we are closer to destruction in A.D. 2000 than we were in A.D. 1000, our altered perspective, based on the infinitely-greater complexity of our existence, has removed much of our sense of urgency, our conviction that we shall be judged in the hereafter, and the belief that such judgment is imminent.

Think about our own century—from what we've experienced, read about, or heard about from those who came before us, we can in our minds divide the decades: the Twenties—the invention of radio, a booming stock market, mass-produced automobiles; the Thirties—the Talkies, the Great Depression, the rise of Fascism; the Forties—the world goes to war, women enter the work force in great numbers, the birth of the Atomic Era; the Fifties—television comes of age, Sputnik, the Cold War; the Sixties—the Cuban missile crisis, the assassinations of Dr. Martin Luther King, Jr., Senator Robert F. Kennedy, and President John F. Kennedy, the escalation of the war in Vietnam; the Seventies—Watergate, the American hostage crisis in Iran, the rise of international terrorism; the Eighties—Japanese technology, AIDS, and the collapse of the Berlin Wall.

And yet, even with the apparently easy separation of our century into decades characterized by different mind-sets, attitudes, and events, the flapper of the Twenties raised her son in the hard-times Thirties, saw him go off to fight in the Forties, and become a grandmother in the Fifties of children she didn't understand in the Sixties and Seventies.

The point I'm making is that time keeps flowing in one uninterrupted line, yet it is punctuated by events of importance, which are influenced by previous events and which in turn influence later events. Nothing stands alone; no event is isolated from the others. Your understanding of this will greatly increase your power of perspective and your understanding of the world, both the outside world and the one within yourself. Remember the maxim about those who don't profit from the mistakes of history being condemned to repeat them. In the same way, those who don't profit from their mistakes in life are condemned to repeat them.

EXERCISE

Draw up a specific time line of your own, without reference to anything but memories of your own life. Place on it everything of importance that has happened to you so far—anything of some significance to you. Individual dates are not important—only the sequence of events.

EXERCISE

When your time line is correct, superimpose it on the time line of historical events in the same year and/or decade. Everyone who experienced the assassination of President John F. Kennedy can say where he/she was and what he/she was doing when the news broke. Try to recall where you were and what the *world* was doing during every event on your own time line.

BRAIN BUILDER #142

PUT THE PAST INTO PERSPECTIVE.

Exercise: Now that you have the order of events in sequence, start associating the events I've given you on the time line on page 218 with the time period in which they occurred. Picture each event as having an influence and effect on following events, and try to perceive what those influences and effects were.

Go over the time line again, just a few more times, until you know generally in which century every event took place. Again, this is not a lesson in history, but in perspective. What and how much you remember is not as important as your increased sense of historical perspective.

Exercise: Choose an epochal event, such as the war in Vietnam. Without being too demanding of yourself about dates, picture the time line of events that led directly to it, and what events flowed from it. In other words, put the Vietnam War into perspective. Or choose a more scientific event, such as the invention of television. What earlier inventions and forward steps in technology led directly to its development? How far back in time can you carry your event? How far forward?

Exercise: Choose an event in your own life, something you remember clearly, whether happily or sadly. Try to see it in the perspective of your own history. What events led up to it? Which events led away from it? Was the event inevitable or preventable? If the event was the result of a mistake on your part, have you made that mistake again? If it was a joyous or successful event for you, have you managed to repeat that success or experience that joy again? Are you aware of the components of that success? What have you learned from your epochal event?

BRAIN BUILDER #143

PUT THE PRESENT INTO PERSPECTIVE.

The American colonies were established on the principles of religious freedom, but on a Christian form of worship. Americans who practice their religion have a tendency to believe that Christianity is the dominant world religion. Because Christians evangelize, they have spread Christianity to the far corners of the globe and imposed the Gregorian calendar on most of the world. Officially, when it's 1990 in the Christian world, it's 1990 just about everywhere else, even in the People's Republic of China, where the Gregorian calendar was adopted as late as 1949. But the adoption of a universal calendar was not based on the dominance of Christianity; it was for convenience in an increasingly complicated world in which communication is now nearly immediate and the globe itself has "shrunk."

A Good Example of Bad Perspective

This American belief in the worldwide dominance of Christianity is an almost-perfect example of false perspective. Just read the following facts.

ONE COMPARISON OF WORLD RELIGIONS

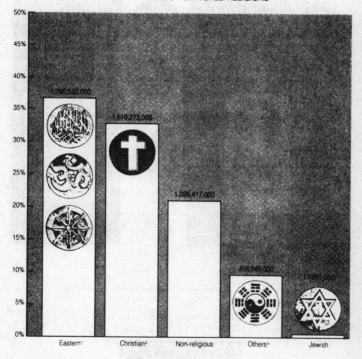

'(includes Muslim, Hindu, Buddhist)
²(includes Roman Catholic, Protestant, Orthodox)
³(includes Folk Religion, New Religion, Sikh, Shaman, Confucian, Baha'i, Shinto, Jain)

(From 1987 ENCYCLOPAEDIA BRITANNICA BOOK OF THE YEAR)

The two graphs (above and on page 224) speak for themselves; need we say much more? Christianity doesn't dominate by reason of its numbers; the Eastern religions have at least 17,000,000 more adherents. The lesson of this chapter in *Brain Power*—and the following chapter—is one of the most important in this book.

ANOTHER COMPARISON OF WORLD RELIGIONS

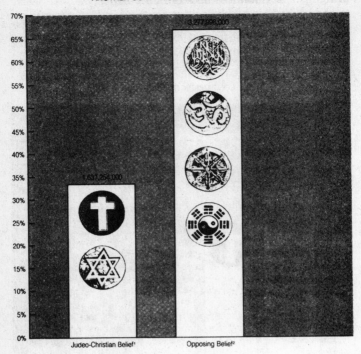

*(includes Roman Catholic, Protestant, Orthodox , Jew)

²(includes Muslim, Hindu, Buddhist, Non-religious, Folk Religion, New Religion, Sikh, Shaman, Confucian, Baha'i, Shinto, Jain)

(From 1987 ENCYCLOPAEDIA BRITANNICA BOOK OF THE YEAR)

EXERCISE

If you're a Christian, read the section on Judaism in your encyclopedia. If you're a Jew, read the section on Christianity.

Having discussed a historical perspective and a religious perspective, let's turn to the building of a more personal overview. Gaining a perspective on yourself is crucial to your intellectual functioning, but your sociocultural upbringing and milieu can stand in your way. You must learn to shed it before you die as just another soldier in someone else's war.

BRAIN BUILDER #144

GAIN NEW PERSPECTIVE FROM THE PERSPECTIVES OF OTHERS.

Where you stand often determines what you see and how you see it. An obvious case is a Seurat painting, composed entirely of tiny dots of color in a technique known as "pointillism." If you stand with your nose against the painting known as "Sunday in the Park," all you'll see is dots. But if you step away from it, beauty begins to emerge—stately figures of men and women, lovely flowers, a river, a sweeping lawn, children playing. Magically, the dots of color turn into a work of art.

In life, it's often necessary to step back in order to see the pattern emerge, and the perspective of others can be of immeasurable help in building your own. Don't confuse this Brain Builder with allowing other people to do your thinking for you. The most independent thinkers are often those who open their minds to the minds of others.

When a friend of mine was nineteen years old, she enrolled in a required college course in English literature. She had already read every book and poem on the course syllabus, some of them more than once, and she knew she would pull an A, perhaps even an A+. On the first day of class, she looked around herself a little smugly and disdainfully. What could these other students have to contribute to her understanding? Could they possibly be as well-read as she? Never.

The class was an eye-opener. As each work was read and discussed, my friend discovered that, while her perspective on it was a good one, sometimes even a brilliant one, it was by no means the only valid one. Almost every other student in the class had something useful and insightful to contribute, a new approach and perspective that had never occurred to my friend. It was a healthy blow to an unhealthily closed-off perspective, and it taught my friend a valuable lesson in life—always be receptive to what others have to say, *especially* if their point of view is not like your own. "Well-read" doesn't equate with "wise," and the two shouldn't be confused. Here are some simple, yet effective methods for gaining access to the perspective of others.

BRAIN BUILDER #145

USE THE THOUGHTS OF OTHERS.

Make a conscious effort to admit the perspectives of others to your thinking.

Exercise: Buy a copy of *Bartlett's Familiar Quotations* by John Bartlett (Little, Brown). Every day, read one selection; think about what the writer has written, and apply its wisdom to your everyday life. Add the book to your "intellectual first aid kit"; it's very useful. Don't go through your Bartlett's systematically; instead, open the book to any page and read the first quotation that presents itself to your eye. Read it again, then close the book and think about the words. Try to determine in your mind the author's perspective. Optimistic? Pessimistic? Liberal? Conservative? Does his outlook agree with your own? Can you see the topic in the same way the author of the quotation does? If not, try a little. Do this daily, and a wide range of outlooks will be opened to you.

BRAIN BUILDER #146

SEE THROUGH THE EYES OF ANOTHER.

Become truly familiar with the perspective of one other person. Remember that political rally (of the *other* party) we sent you to in the last chapter? Where you were supposed to keep your mouth shut?

Exercise: Go back again, to another rally or meeting, and *open* your mouth this time, but in a constructive way. Talk to people; get to know them and what they're thinking.

Exercise: Every day for a week, read the same poem. The purest purpose of poetry is to unveil to the reader a familiar sight to look at in an unfamiliar way, to find the new in the old. The poet's perspective is unlike any other; it is unique and wonderful, and this is one of the most pleasurable of the Brain Building exercises.

Select a poem—excellent sources are *The Viking Book of Poetry* and the Oxford University Press collections of American verse and British verse—and read it every day for a week, until you are completely familiar with the poet's perspective. How has it differed from your own?

Here's a good example of what I mean. Suppose you select as your poem-of-the-week John Keats's "Ode on a Grecian Urn." If you read this poem every day for a week, you will not only be experiencing beauty and opening your mind to wonder, you will be sharing Keats's own outlook on the face of beauty. After you've read the poem five or six times, go to your local art museum and look only at a piece of Attic pottery from the fifth century B.C. If there isn't one in the museum's collections, do the next best thing: Go to your library and look at a volume of pictures of ancient Greek vases; many books contain beautiful color plates of Attic vases. A "Grecian urn" like these was the poet's inspiration for the ode.

As you study the vases or the pictures, even if you've seen Greek vases just like them before, you will find that your perspective has changed. You will be seeing through Keats's eyes. You will have absorbed Keats's poetic vision and added enormous treasures to the richness of your intellect. Then read the poem once or twice more, and you will be reading it from a new perspective.

Now, having tasted the sublime, let's turn to the everyday.

BRAIN BUILDER #147

BE YOUR OWN PARENT; BE YOUR OWN CHILD.

When children are small, their parents tend to think that everything that comes out of their rosebud mouths is adorable, intelligent, precious, and worth repeating endlessly. Then the kids become older, and suddenly, parents are not giving credence to anything they say; parents have lost respect for their children in the same way that children, who once thought Mommy and Daddy were the experts of the Western world, have now lost respect for their parents. Let's examine this change of perspective and how to improve it. This will work equally well whether you're a parent, a child, or both.

Exercise: Try to view yourself from your parents' perspective if you're the child; your child's, if you're the parent. When you're stating your case about something, is your tone of voice worthy of respect? Are you imparting information or explaining your feelings in a rational way, or is your tone emotion-loaded, subsconsiously designed to trigger an equally emotional response? Are you prepared to be challenged or contradicted, or is your stance that you are in the absolute right and that nothing anybody can say or do will change your mind?

Are you clean, decently dressed, your hair combed neatly? This is not a joke; it's very difficult to take someone in pajamas seriously or to accept counsel from someone who's just asked you for a loan.

Parents vs. Children: Does Familiarity Breed Contempt?

The years roll by, and the kids get older. Suddenly, their parents no longer think they're budding geniuses. Why? Why do parents tend to treat children as though they know nothing? Is it because the children behave as if they know everything?

Actually, familiarity does tend to breed a little contempt. Even when you're an adult, parents still see you as their child, but see other adults as the adults they are, even though those other adults are seen as children by their parents! The problem is that they lack perspective. They still perceive you as a child, but since you do not continue to do childish things (presumably), they don't find you cute any more.

It produces rage to see your parents accepting statements and opinions of others while degrading your own. If you pass off a statement of your own as coming from someone else, they may very well nod their acceptance!

In other words, parents often tend to respect the intelligence only of other people's children!

On the other hand, sons and daughters tend to regress to more childish behavior around their parents, aware that fault is always being found with them. It's a difficult situation, but a common one, and it's highly doubtful that you'll ever get to change this state of affairs. People who lack perspective cannot have it forced upon them. The best thing you can do is to accept the situation and to come prepared for it. Hold onto your positive self-image with both hands and never let it out of your sight. Better yet, don't make this same grave mistake with your own children.

In order to be accepted for what you are, you may have to deal with people who don't know you and who can therefore maintain perspective about you. This may be a shocking realization, but it's a healthy one. Unless you have a most unusual set of parents, parents with perspective, or unless you have a particularly hardy self-image, the longer you remain in an intimate surrounding, the less likely it is that your intellect will come to full fruition.

That's the reason so many people "leave home," moving from the cities or the areas in which they were born. They are searching for the respect they can't get from "their people," while they know they can get it from strangers. On the other hand, many people remain trapped in their familiar environment and intellectually stunted. They believe the negative assessment of them; it becomes a self-fulfilling prophecy.

It might be necessary for you to leave, but before you do, before you give up all the positive aspects of family, try these exercises in gaining perspective:

EXERCISE

Begin to treat family members more impersonally, as you would business associates. You wouldn't expect a client or fellow-worker to respect your opinion if you presented it in your nightgown. Dress and behave with dignity at home. Step back and see the picture you're presenting of yourself, just as you would in business. Try to refrain from using terms like "Mom" and "Dad" that trigger memories of childhood. If you say "Mommy" and "Daddy," you're asking for babying, not respect.

EXERCISE

Don't become emotional with your parents; you wouldn't do it with a client or coworker. You wouldn't shout at a client, "You never listen to anything I say!"

EXERCISE

Show confidence in yourself. You know that you must exhibit self-confidence around business associates. Begin to do this around your parents. It's the key to success. Interestingly enough, the longer you are self-confident, the more your parents will respect you, and the less you will be concerned if they do.

BRAIN BUILDER #148

SEE YOURSELF THROUGH THE EYES OF YOUR LOVED ONES.

Gain perspective on your relationship with your husband or wife or with your children. Look at yourself through their eyes. Your marriage partner is probably the closest you're going to come to an intellectual equal who is also an intimate. This person has made a commitment to you. You may have friends who are your equals, but how many of them would marry you? Your wife or husband is the person to whom you should look for intellectual support in the immediate family. However, if she or he is your *sole* intellectual support, you're in a fix. What if your spouse becomes less and less supportive over the years? Worse, what if you progress beyond him or her? What becomes of support when people are far apart?

Your children, over the space of twenty years or less, move from being adoring and adorable little sycophants to being relentlessly resistant to the benefit of your experience. This often sparks the beginning of lifelong estrangement.

Your friends usually play the role of intellectual equalizer. They seldom urge you upward; they are afraid of losing you if you outstrip them. Instead, they urge you toward them. The longer you let them do this, the more like them you'll become. Assuming this is so, step back and take a look at your friends. Are these the people you want to be like?

Exercise: Answer these questions as honestly as possible:

Does your husband or wife truly respect you?

Do all of your children respect you?

Does your mother respect you?

Does your father respect you?

Do all of your friends respect you?

Do you deserve respect?

If you deserve respect, but you're not getting it, you might consider spending more time with those who respect you and less time with those who don't.

SEE YOURSELF THROUGH THE EYES OF YOUR
COWORKERS AND EMPLOYERS.

Exercise: Go through your desk at the office and either
throw out everything that looks silly or take it home. That
includes the stuffed animal with the crossed eyes, the mug
that says something sarcastic, and the poster with the kitten
out on a limb that reads "Hang in There." If your environment indicates that you don't take yourself seriously, nobody else will.

Consider how you look to your employer or your immediate superior at work. How do you think you look when you
bite into a cookie at your desk? How do you think you look
when you brush your hair or fix your makeup in public?
Like a person worth taking seriously? Would you come to
work in your bathrobe? No, you dress with dignity for the
office, but you can ruin the dignity by snippets of personal
behavior that are out of place, and because of which, consciously or unconsciously, others pin labels on you.

As you view yourself through others' eyes, you begin to
learn how to escape the labels that others have pinned on
you, and more importantly, *labels that you have unconsciously pinned on yourself.*

The strong possibility exists that you're giving people the
ammunition they can use against you. Example: If you're a
woman, are you wearing decorative bows, especially in your
hair? If you do, do you expect to be regarded as equal to a
man in the same job? Ribbon bows are associated with being
a little girl, not a mature and responsible woman. Unconsciously, others will label you lightweight.

Another example: Do you use nonstandard grammar and
street slang? If so, you, too, regardless of your capabilities
and intelligence, will be labeled lightweight.

Be your own best intellectual support, not your own subconscious detractor. *When you can see yourself, you can see
everyone.*

BROADEN THE SCOPE OF YOUR PERSPECTIVE.

Exercise: Write a one-page, off-the-cuff essay about yourself without categorizing yourself by saying what you do for a living or whether you're a parent or where you go to church or whether you're a man or woman or black or white.

All brilliance might be funneled into one area alone, while other areas remain shut off. A Nobel Prize winner may be a genius in his field, but an ignoramus in all others. Often, the more time an expert spends in his field, the less time he has to learn about anything else.

Why do people funnel their intelligence? There are various valid reasons: a need to concentrate their energies on a monumental work-in-progress or perhaps a deep involvement—intellectual and/or emotional—with the problem at hand. But sometimes people funnel because they are passive and would rather retreat into an ivory tower of the mind than confront the chaos of the world.

This needn't be the case with you. You must continually question your approach to matters. How broad is your thinking? Am I thinking like a *(fill in your own profession here)*? Like a parent? Like a *(fill in your religious belief here)*? Like a *(man or woman)*?

Build a bridge with your mind, not a tunnel. If you're a carpenter, you must think like one while you're working. But that doesn't mean you're forced to think like a carpenter twenty-four hours a day. That's *dependent*, not *independent* thinking. What frame of reference are you using in forming a judgment? Your own? Someone else's? Is your judgment formed from your own life experience or from what you think others think is the right judgment? Do you recognize the influences on you that form your perspective? Let's examine some of these daily influences and how they affect you through a series of Brain Builders.

BRAIN BUILDER #151

DON'T PERMIT FAMILIARITY TO INDUCE
A LOSS OF OBJECTIVITY.

Sometimes things we take for granted have contributed more than we know to slanting our thinking. Here's a very simple example: The annual Academy Awards committee hands out an Oscar to "Best Actor" and "Best Actress." Why?

Should we have an award for "Best White Actor" and "Best Black Actor," or "Best Actress Under 55" and "Best Actress Over 55"? Wouldn't that seem ridiculous? It should, and so should "Best Actor" and "Best Actress," awards separated only by gender. It's a concept we might not dream of instituting today, but one which we accept because we've inherited it from the past and have never given it a second thought. If it was around when we were born, we tend to accept it as a natural part of life. If there were no income tax, would we vote one in? If the British didn't have a monarchy, would they put one on the ballot?

Give It a Second Thought

What can you do to avoid the problem of an unconscious acceptance through familiarity? How can you learn to "give it a second thought" and increase your perspective on yourself and others?

It's a matter of objectivity. We read a newspaper account of a local incident involving a "male Caucasian, age 32," or a "female Hispanic, age about 50," and we unconsciously make judgments and assumptions according to gender, age, race.

Identifying people by gender, age, and race makes us use those as categories for judgments as though they were to blame for everything. Why not list the political party of every person involved, for example? (That might be interesting. Belonging to a political party is voluntary and indicates something about the person's mind.)

Consider how your thinking has been affected by identifying certain behavior with gender, for example, instead of by more pertinent criteria. Stop. Step back. Make a conscious effort to abandon those conceptions and misconceptions. Open your mind; make the familiar unfamiliar again by examining it as though for the first time.

Then examine yourself. How much of your *own* behavior is influenced by what you've been taught to perceive as right or appropriate for your gender and age, etc.

Exercise: Make a list of the aspects of a person that you think would be more illustrative of the situation than his or her gender, age, or race.

BRAIN BUILDER #152

TAKE A CLOSER LOOK AT ADVERTISING.

Life, alas, is not all Keats. Most of it is just day-to-day stuff, and much of the fabric of modern American life contains advertising—on radio, on television, and in print. Learn to look at it from a new perspective. Does anything look that good in real life? That beautiful model touting hairspray while floating around in sheer chiffon and four-inch-heels—if you took away her photogenic hairstyle (which is blown about so becomingly not by nature, but by a wind machine), her makeup, including all the eyelashes and fake contours and lipstick, the cosmetic surgery that altered her nose, chin, and cheekbones, the artful lighting, and the softening filters used on the camera lens, would she be just as beautiful?

Is it as much fun to hang out in your neighborhood bar as it is in the jolly, convivial places full of good-looking men and women pictured in the beer commercials? Is your automobile as exciting and inspirational to drive as the ads suggest, with their shot-from-a-helicopter-above photography?

Don't let TV commercials or other advertising get at you subliminally. Ask yourself: Does this ad make me feel worse about myself? Am I expected to believe I'm not smart enough, attractive enough, or *anything* enough?

Exercise: For the next two weeks, keep that hand-held mirror nearby while you're watching television. Once each evening, during a commercial, pick it up and take a good look at your face. Does the advertising pitch make you feel better about yourself? Or worse? How do you think this has been affecting you over the years? Practice this perspective; it is an extremely valuable tool in dealing with others in daily life. It gives you a chance to step back and listen to the real meaning of others' words. Are those words trying to make you feel worse about yourself? Have you been letting them? And is it true, or is it just a way of separating you from your money?

BRAIN BUILDER #153

SET UP YOUR OWN "I" RATING FOR THE MOVIES YOU SEE.

Have you ever, while watching a film, said to yourself: "Why don't *I* ever run across anybody that great-looking? I've never even *seen* one in person. Where *are* all these gorgeous people, anyway?"

I'll tell you where—they're on the sets and inside the film studios. And they are wearing thousands of dollars' worth of makeup artistry, hairstyling technique, special lighting, and hype. Without all those things, you wouldn't even recognize them. At the very least, they'd lose all their glamor.

When I said you had to develop an "I" rating for movies, I meant "I" for Intelligence, and "I" for yourself. *Do not go to films that damage your own self-image.*

The worst are films that purport to entertain you, but that actually leave you depressed or dissatisfied, unhappy with yourself and your life. Included in this group are:

1) Films that depict personal relationships in an artificial manner, so that you long for a relationship as spontaneously romantic in your own life. Life is cruel to the romantic. There are people who, after seeing *Gone with the Wind*, will never be satisfied with their own relationship, no matter how fulfilling. They want to be Rhett Butler and Scarlett O'Hara. There will always be a silent, usually unconscious, comparison.

2) Movies that glamorize or beautify life-styles that in real life are actually sordid. Take *Night Shift*, for example. It portrays a group of clean, young, well-spoken, altogether adorable prostitutes. There's no disease, drug addiction, or crime.

On the other hand, there are films which do no damage to your intellectual strength or self-image. These are the escapist movies that make no pretense at reality, but instead advertise only entertainment. In that category are broad comedies like *Airplane!*, broad stylized fantasies such as *Star Wars*, broad adventure stories like *Jewel of the Nile*, broad musicals that don't romanticize, such as *Singin' in the Rain*, and cartoons with no hidden messages such as Disney's *Fantasia*.

And, finally, there are films which may actually strengthen your intellectual power by giving you something real and valuable to think about. Among them are such "I-rated" motion pictures as:

1) Unglamorized movies that give you an insight into the human condition, such as *Come Back, Little Sheba*, and *On Golden Pond.*

2) Realistic movies that take you to places and happenings you might otherwise never see, such as *All Quiet on the Western Front* and *Platoon.*

Don't waste your money on anything that wastes your precious time or erodes your self-confidence or sets up false expectations no one can ever meet. And don't be afraid to walk out on a movie that you discover won't do anything for you. Having wasted your money, don't send your precious time skittering after it.

Exercise: Try an entirely different kind of movie. At least once a month, go out and see a foreign film, preferably one with subtitles.

BRAIN BUILDER #154

SEE YOURSELF AS STRANGERS DO.

Exercise: Pay special attention to the way people you see are dressed. Make a judgment about each one. What can you tell from their clothing? Are they liberal or conservative? Rich or poor? Desirable or undesirable? Then realize that you are being judged in the same way by them, whether consciously or unconsciously. Step back and try to make the same judgment that others would.

Remember what I said earlier, *When you can see yourself, you can see everyone.* There's another side to that coin, equally valid. *When you can see everyone else, you can see yourself.* But only if you want to.

A Quiz for the End of Week Eleven

1) Which civilization came first in recorded history: the Egyptians, the Greeks, or the Romans?
2) Who came first, Buddha or Jesus?
3) What do these dates refer to: 1066, 1775, 1861, 1914, 1939?
4) Which came first, the Black Death or the Great Fire of London?
5) What are the followers of the three major Eastern religions called?
6) Is the great majority of the world's population Christian?
7) Are the nonreligous only a tiny minority?
8) What fraction of the world's population is Jewish?
9) What was that book of quotations I recommended?
10) Can you now improve that definition of intelligence you wrote down weeks ago?

Answers

1) The Egyptians first, then the Greeks, and then the Romans.
2) Buddha.
3) The Battle of Hastings, the American Revolution, the American Civil War, World War I, World War II.
4) The plague began in 1347 A.D.; the Great Fire of London burned in 1666 A.D.
5) Muslims, Hindus, and Buddhists.
6) No. Only about a third are Christian.
7) No. About a fifth have no religion at all.
8) Only about half a percent.
9) *Bartlett's Familiar Quotations* by John Bartlett.
10) I certainly hope so!

CHAPTER

15

WEEK TWELVE

| M | T | W | T | F | S | S |

The Well-Built Mind

To regard anyone except yourself as responsible for your judgment is to be a slave, not a free man. It is from this fact that the liberal arts acquire their name.

—Mortimer J. Adler and Charles Van Doren

Together you and I have made a long and difficult journey to get to this final chapter. In guiding you to build your intellectual power, I've required you to abandon conventional ways of thinking, re-examine all your most cherished beliefs, and above all, let go of your previously-held conclusions because most of our conclusions aren't ours at all. They come from others—our families, the media, the church, and the state.

I've shown you how to open your mind to the infinite possibilities of new ideas, how to use valuable intellectual tools such as logic, vocabulary, and attention span, how to sharpen your own innate powers of comprehension, insight, intuition, and sensory perception, how to develop confidence in your own mental abilities, separate the wheat of truth from the chaff of mere opinion, and build your brain to use power thinking instead.

Now, I'll give you one last Brain Builder, the key to power thinking. Power thinking embraces reality rather than tradition, takes nothing for granted, is open-ended, and what is more, it's a cognitive leap beyond what's most commonly known as "critical thinking." Power thinking is *leading-edge thinking.*

BRAIN BUILDER #155

PRACTICE POWER THINKING BY BEING AWARE WHENEVER
YOU "DRAW A CONCLUSION."

Power thinking recognizes no limits. *Your conclusions are your limits.*

Exercise: Take a look at the list below. Have you drawn conclusions about any of them?

Strategic Defense Initiative

aid to the Contras

the budget deficit

Now look back at the list. Can you honestly say you really *know* a great deal about the things about which you drew conclusions? But just because you *draw* a conclusion doesn't mean you can't *erase* it!

Rebuilding That Old Framework

Consider the child. He gets his first ideas at an early age and absorbs them, repeating the process as he forms a rapidly hardening frame of reference. With the passage of time, he proceeds to fit new information into that old framework, often cramming it in sideways and ignoring what doesn't fit in at all. He uses what he has learned in the past to understand and assimilate what he learns in the present. And if what he learned in the past is not true, his present "learning" is skewed to those errors.

We are those children. Grown up.

We received a lot more from our parents than we would like to believe. We got our brains from the gene pool of humankind, but only a couple of people, more or less, proceeded to fill it. What we believed when we were five was dependent on what we absorbed those first four years. And what we believed when we were ten was dependent on what we absorbed those first nine years. If step five was weak, I wouldn't want to be setting foot on step twenty-five.

A lot of what we absorbed made sense, but a great deal of it made "non-sense." This is one of the reasons intellectual progress is so slow.

Given the circumstances of our upbringing, it's almost as if we've been held hostage; we learned things involuntarily from those who had power and authority over us. As we grow older, however, the situation changes to voluntary. In other words, we have an excuse for our errors only up to about the age of twenty or twenty-five. After that, we have only ourselves to thank or blame.

As we grow older, it seems to matter less that our ideas are accurate than it does that they are ours. We've become accustomed to them and therefore somehow find them comforting. From them we receive a measure of security, even if false security. Is it any wonder then that we defend our ideas against all challengers? This defense, this intellectual tension, is very detrimental to our overall mental functioning because we've drawn conclusions.

Just think for a moment about what that means—"drawing a conclusion." Why should we ever draw a conclusion to our thinking process? Why should we ever stop thinking? And when do we know enough to draw a conclusion to our thinking? The answer should be "never."

I don't like the word "conclusion" even when it's modified by a word such as "preliminary" because "conclusion" still means "end" to me. The very concept doesn't make sense; it's an oxymoron—how can it be preliminary

241

and still a conclusion? In my life, I've seen too many people who came to an end in their thinking—about one thing or lots of things—five years or twenty-five years or even fifty years ago! But even five minutes ago doesn't make it right. (All those other conclusions were five minutes old at some point, too.)

The most crucial step you should have mastered by now in Brain Building is perhaps the hardest: admitting that you have made errors, can make errors, do make errors, and will make errors. Everybody accepts this in theory, but practice is too often another matter entirely. Yet, admitting mistakes is at the very heart of really solid intellectual functioning. A positive side effect is an increase in your popularity; people really seem to love somebody who confesses to erring.

Parenthetically, it's relatively easy to admit errors you make today or will make tomorrow. What really separates the men and women from the boys and girls is admitting the errors in thinking that you've *already* made. And that means telling *yourself* that you're wrong—possibly the hardest confession of all.

But cheer up. The admission of error might be classified as a failure, but *change on that basis is called improvement*. The process is ongoing, like the automobile. The first automobile was slow, uncomfortable and so filthy to ride in that people wore linen dusters over their clothing. But it was hardly a failure; it was the first step toward outstanding success.

Power thinking is not based on "opinion. The word is a crutch, spoken merely to lend dignity to groundless thinking. People who have no reasonable means of intellectual support say, "I have a right to my opinion." Don't you be one of them.

I've never been impressed by people who claim loudly that they have "the courage of their convictions." After all, there are people today who walk around claiming to be the son of God. They have the courage of their convictions, too. It's not the courage of convictions I admire, it's the accuracy, and that accuracy only comes from a diligent pursuit of the truth.

Remember this: your intellectual ability can be described

as your ability to distinguish, to a finer and finer degree, sense from non-sense.

The well-built mind is open, not shut. It seeks to refine information into the truth, to deal with ideas, not "conclusions" or "opinions." The well-built mind has dispensed with misconceptions, preconceptions, and even postconceptions. The well-built mind is eager to meet others like it, *whether they agree or not.*

The well-built mind welcomes a refreshing discussion, disagreement and all, without arguing. The well-built mind is aware of the world's infinite possibilities and reaches out in every direction. The well-built mind takes full responsibility for itself and its ideas and actions; it is objective, seeking only for reality and improvement, rejecting complacency and excuses.

The well-built mind is a confident, growing, totally alive entity, with an expanding potential and a limitless future.

And it can be yours.

Also from Piatkus:

CHANGE YOUR BRAIN, CHANGE YOUR LIFE

The breakthrough programme for conquering anger, anxiety and depression

Daniel Amen

In this breakthrough US bestseller, you'll see scientific evidence that your anxiety, depression, anger, obsessiveness or impulsiveness could be related to how specific structures in your brain work.

Pioneering neuropsychiatrist Dr Daniel Amen provides convincing evidence that many problems formerly considered psychological, such as anxiety and depression, actually have a biological basis. The good news is that you're not stuck with the brain you're born with. In this ground-breaking book, Dr Amen offers a wealth of surprising – and effective – 'brain prescriptions' that can help heal your brain and change your life.

Dr Daniel G Amen is a clinical neuroscientist, psychiatrist, Distinguished Fellow of the American Psychiatric Association and CEO of Amen clinics, Inc, in the USA. He is a recognised expert on the relationship between the brain and behaviour and is the author of several books.

'Revolutionary. Dr Amen shows how your brain can become your worst enemy, and, with the proper treatment, your best friend'
Dr Martin Stein, associate clinical professor of psychiatry, George Washington University

'A book by the pioneer of functional brain scans – at last, some science in the fuzzy world of mental health diagnosis'
Professor Jane Plant, CBE DSc FRSM FRSE, co-author of *Beating Stress, Anxiety and Depression*

978-0-7499-4191-8